I0790891

OUT OF THE SILENCE

My Journey into Post-traumatic Stress Disorder and Back

HOWARD LOVELY JR

Foreword by Mark Russell, Ph.D.

BALBOA.
PRESS

A DIVISION OF HAY HOUSE

Balboa Press books may be ordered through booksellers or by contacting:

Balboa Press
A Division of Hay House
1663 Liberty Drive
Bloomington, IN 47403
www.balboapress.com
1 (877) 407-4847

Print information available on the last page.

ISBN: 978-1-9822-1241-4 (sc)
ISBN: 978-1-9822-1240-7 (hc)
ISBN: 978-1-9822-1242-1 (e)

Library of Congress Control Number: 2018911081

Balboa Press rev. date: 12/16/2019

Dedication

To my parents Martha Leona Lovely (Jackson), in memoriam Howard Lovely, Staff Sergeant 1st class, US Army retired (Veteran of WWII, Korea & Vietnam) and to all my ancestors who may have mentally suffered an untreated ailment similar to mine, via the brutality of slavery and Jim-Crow-South. Thank you for all the things you did that aided my development into the man that I have become. Thank you for showing & teaching me how to survive under some of the most challenging times that the past two centuries threw at both of you (parents) and my ancestors. It is Mom and Dad's courage, skills, creativity, intelligence and perseverance that is deeply embedded within my spirit,… it drives me forward each day.

In memoriam to Great-Grand Mother Doris Tate (Native American), Grand-Mother Ethel Leona Tate & Grand-Daddy Charles Andrew Jackson who was the son of an African slave (Great-Grand-Mother Fannie Jackson born 1859 in Rutledge, TN). Mom's dad was born in the late eighteen-hundred's and lived well into the 1980's,… Grand-Daddy Jackson was just as robust as the swisher-sweet cigars and apple scented pipe tobacco that I remember the smell of him smoking. He was a stately combination of confidence, business minded, family oriented and gentle. Thus he taught me to have a can-do-attitude and humility no matter what.

In memoriam to Grand-Daddy Bert Lovely who was a farmer & Grand-Mother Mamie Upshaw, Dad's parents. Grand-Mother Upshaw taught me the respectful use of extreme power via words & presence that can emanate from a physical body that has betrayed itself. As family matriarch,… she displayed uncompromised dignity and humility as arthritis ravaged her body for no less than 10 years.

To my nieces & nephews, this is my letter to you,… an accounting of a chain of events,… that I trust will offer some explanation rather than an excuse, to my estrangement. It is my deepest desire that as you read this 19 chapter letter, it will shed light on my despicable journey and painfully dark absence from your lives during the past several decades. The profound severity of having missed many of you grow up, is indescribable with words,… and the precipitating actions of which, should not be replicated within your respective families from this point forward.

The generationally passed on, self-destructive pattern, must be broken,… and thus, not allowed residence within your individual homes. This is not a request,… it's a warning.

Acknowledgments

The writing of this book has been often times difficult and definitely emotionally painful; moreover, I've had to learn how to properly assemble a book while simultaneously writing it under a type of duress.

In memoriam, thanks to Frederick Douglass,… my hero and mentor who taught me via his writings, to boldly speak the unspeakable at an inconvenient time, continue to persevere when the odds are clearly against me and dare to give voice to myself and others. He encourages me to have the audacity to confront any oppressive force (physical or mental) with all my intellectual resources.

Thanks to Suzanne & Robert Murray, owners of Style-Matters. They diligently helped me to professionally assemble the book-proposal.

Thanks to all tax paying United States Citizens & Residents who's money,… via the Veterans Administration administered monthly monetary compensation, has for many years provided me with shelter, food, clothing, college education and has also allowed me to finance necessary elements that lead to the writing of this book.

Thanks to each of the following schools and staff / educators, one of which was my aunt (Margaret Lovely), for providing me with a solid basic public education with the minimal resources that were available. Their diligence and professional ability to transfer into my young mind what they knew, has allowed me to write this book to the best of my ability at this time:

Eastport Elementary (closed), Fairgarden Elementary, Park Junior High (closed) and Austin-East High all located in Knoxville Tennessee.

Thank you Russell Wilkie, MFT for taking the time to really "see" and hear me as I told you about my experiences. Then and only then,…

did you choose to accurately make a determination of what challenge(s) or diagnosis that I was confronted with.

Thank you Francine Shapiro (18 Feb. 1948 – 16 June 2019) for creating the EMDR technique and for recommending Mark Russell to write my forward to this book.

Contents

Foreword

Socially estranged, demoralized, and exhausted from incessant suffering of an undiagnosed traumatic stress injury—27-year-old Howard, a single, African American male and U.S. Air Force Airman—attempts suicide. For Howard, and countless others, suicide represented a "final solution": a permanent, violent end to a private misery from unrelenting, uncontrollable, and intensely agonizing "adrenaline rushes" that began in childhood after repeatedly bearing witness to bloody hand-to-hand combat between his parents within the sanctuary of home. Contrary to popular belief, suicide is rarely an impulsive, unpreventable, decision- and can be a reassertion of power versus a posture of surrender. Tragically, this is an all too common outcome for individuals tormented by chronic stress injuries like PTSD, a life-altering condition defined by loss of control over one's mind and body, with its hallmark intrusive and distressful re-experiencing symptoms (i.e., nightmares, recollections), reflexive avoidance (i.e., emotional numbing, social withdrawal), and the unpredictable triggering of hyper-arousal (e.g., exaggerated startle, insomnia, hyper-vigilance) symptoms.

National Mental Health Crisis

Howard's traumatic stress injury was not born from the fires of war, but within the sanctity of home. If national leaders are so brazenly complicit to routinely neglect the mental health needs of its warrior class, what of the rest of society?-especially amongst its most vulnerable, invisible, and less-privileged members-children, adolescents, and the socioeconomically disenfranchised. In the U.S., 1 of 5 children and 1 of 4 adults suffers from mental illness; suicide is third leading cause of death in young adults; massacres like Newtown spark outrage over a deeply flawed mental health system, yet meaningful reforms are missing-in-action. Annually, there are over 700,000 confirmed child abuse cases; 3.3 to 10 million children witness interpersonal violence; 40 to 60% will have behavioral problems such as anxiety, depression, and aggression, indicating the urgent need for early identification and intervention; 3 million women are physically abused by their husband or boyfriend; 85% of domestic violence victims are women, from all races and income status; however, people with lower annual income (below $25K) have a three-times higher risk; 25 to 30% of adults entering the military are trauma survivors, who like Howard, never received adequate mental health services.

Critical Need for Early Identification and Treatment

There is broad expert consensus that early identification and treatment of traumatic stress injuries is critical to prevent long-term neurophysiological injury and disability. Therefore, all children, adolescents, and adults screened and diagnosed with traumatic stress injury should have ready unfettered access to the top "evidence-based" psychotherapies available for stress injuries like PTSD. A key principle in developmental neurobiology is that the brain develops and organizes as a reflection of experience. The neurophysiological activation seen during acute stress in a child is usually rapid and reversible. However, when the stressful event is of a sufficient duration, intensity, or frequency, the brain is altered. Yet despite widespread general knowledge of the potential adverse impact of trauma on developing minds and bodies, less than 1/3 of young survivors receive proper assessment or treatment until many years, often decades of aftermath, later and typically only after a crisis. Of course, children and the poor are not alone in their struggle to receive adequate mental healthcare.

The current wars have ignited another preventable military mental health crisis due largely to the military's repetitive failure to learn from its own well-documented psychiatric lessons of war, including the need to ensure veterans have access to an adequate supply of well-trained specialists using the best available PTSD treatments. However the Veteran's Administration (VA) and the Department of Defense (DoD) have chosen politics over fulfilling its sacred pledge to ensure universal access to best available PTSD treatments-blacklisting the very treatment that Howard reported had saved his life-Eye Movement Desensitization and Reprocessing (EMDR). EMDR is identified by every domestic and international scientific body of PTSD experts, including the VA / DoD (2004/2010) as one of a handful of evidence-based therapies. Unlike standard talk therapy, EMDR does not require vivid, repeated self-disclosures, compliance with 40-60 hours of homework, or expensive virtual reality software. Yet, despite billions of dollars researching every conceivable alternative, the VA and DoD refuses to conduct a single EMDR trial during the past 12 war years! Moreover, with impunity, the VA forces veterans to choose between two homegrown talk therapies, excluding EMDR. How many thousands of veterans might have been saved like Howard? Would this be allowed if vets were barred from a proven potentially life-saving surgical procedure?

Linking the National and Military Mental Health Crises

Howard's poignant story clearly transcends the mental health crises in the military and broader society, mirroring the experiences of millions of underserved Americans betrayed by a failed national leadership, unwilling to transform the current antiquated mental health system. It's through personal narratives like Howard's, that Western society may finally end the exorbitantly harmful and costly policies of disparity, by embracing the truth that mental, physical, social, and spiritual human dimensions are inseparable, invaluable, and equal determinants of illness and health. At this time, only a concerted congressional effort to investigate and fix the preventable causes of the current military mental health crisis will offer an adequate national model needed to transport the American mental health system into the 21st century.

Mark C. Russell, Ph.D., ABPP, Commander, U.S. Navy (Retired)
Chair, Psy.D. Program, Antioch University Seattle

ABPP = Board Certification in Clinical Psychology by the American Board of Professional Psychology

Introduction

When I was 27 years old, I tried to kill myself—because I was tired of the uncontrollable adrenaline rushes that washed over my body and that made my skin crawl every day. I was tired of simply "mushing" through life. And I was definitely tired of playing the pretend game. I was tired of putting on the smile, the shined up boots, and the pressed military uniform and acting like everything was alright….it wasn't. Everything was, in fact, all wrong. Since I was eight years old, I had been waking every morning with soaked sheets—not because I had wet the bed, but because I was sweating my way through nightmare after nightmare. During daylight hours, my body was being continually tricked and triggered into full-on attack mode, as if I had to fight or run for my life. Sometimes, the events that triggered these adrenaline rushes involved people being unkind or even cruel to me—like the taunts I suffered at the hands of my fellow service members—but others were normal acts that occurred throughout an ordinary day: the sound of a car horn beeping, a friend shouting over to another across the room, and by the end, the sound of a hummingbird flapping its wings or the sound of my own stomach gurgling out of hunger. Even when I quit my job as an airplane structural mechanic (years after being honorably discharged from the military) and I moved away into a cottage in the woods with just my dog, I couldn't escape the anxiety and fear that flooded my body every day. In my garden... In the garage... At the stop light at an intersection. No matter where I was, alone or with other people—family, friend, or foe—an attack of anxiety could arise that made my internal experience of the present environment feel like the world was endlessly (and unjustifiably) attacking me. This chronic, silent, and painful state of existence could be triggered by a simple sound or an unexpected movement like that hummingbird. I looked to my religious and cultural beliefs at the time for some reasonable answer of what was happening to me—the longstanding internal torment that dogged me daily—but there was nothing. I was lost and alone in the valley of the shadow of death, my body feeling as if it were invisibly surrounded by an intangible foe. In fact, I was already "living" a strange "death" because some part of me had died long ago as an 8-year-old boy witnessing his Mom and Dad threaten to kill one another time and time again. When reflecting on the tragic family life that pervaded my youth, I often think of the following anonymous quote: "He who endeavors to kill another, with no regard for the bystander that witnesses the act, has impacted three individuals." If only my parents had known the power of their threats and screams, their taunts and my dad's smacks. The night of my suicide attempt (back when I was still in the military), I had *sixteen* of the possible seventeen symptoms of posttraumatic stress disorder. I didn't know it then but I had developed PTSD many years before, in response to a frightening event I had witnessed in my youth. As a result of my PTSD, I was moving through my life under constant duress, and by the night of my suicide attempt, I had lost the strength to keep on battling. Fortunately, when I hung my belt on a closet rod in a motel I checked into in West Memphis, Arkansas—three states away from my station at an Air Force Base and two nights after going AWOL—and tested the belt out around my neck, my brain generated one of its sensible thoughts. What came to me? "This feels uncomfortable." While contemplating what to do next, I sat back down on the bed for a moment. Then I remembered that I had a Tech Sergeant's phone number in my wallet and I decided to give him a call. "Lovely, is that you, man?" he asked, recognizing my voice instantly on the line. He made me promise that I'd get my butt back to base and in return he would tell everyone I was coming home so I could avoid being pursued and thrown into jail for going AWOL. Years later, when I became a crisis counselor on a suicide hotline, I'd realize that the Sgt. was contracting with me—he was making me promise to come back because he knew I was a man of my word and that that promise to return might stop me from killing myself. I'll never know for sure, but that night, that Sgt. may just have saved my life. I hope that in writing this book, I might be able to save someone else's life, just as that Sgt. may have saved mine that lonely night in a motel in West Memphis. I know from my own years of enduring posttraumatic stress disorder that those who experience it suffer hour by hour, minute by minute, through a living hell. It's a disorder that causes your body to turn on itself—when the very instincts and responses meant to protect you from real harm start firing at the wrong times and set you at war with the world around you as well as with yourself. Sometimes, you grow hyper-vigilant, sure you should watch your back after someone makes a comment or you hear a strange sound. Other times, even though your brain is telling you that you've just heard an everyday sound, your body rushes ahead, heart throbbing, muscles tightening, palms sweating. You tell yourself to calm down—it's just the sound of the wind against the trees or a tired old dog barking—but your body won't listen. Instead, your body's racing you down the rollercoaster of anxiety once again, throwing you into another fit of PTSD.

Today, millions of individuals suffer from posttraumatic stress disorder—*millions!*—and many of them suffer without even knowing it. The disorder tends to be thought of in association with military service, going back to the Vietnam war and has gotten the most coverage lately in relation to the increased numbers of U.S. soldiers who have developed the condition in response to their service in Iraq and Afghanistan. In fact, the U.S. Department of Veterans Affairs indicates that almost 31 percent of Vietnam veterans, as many as 10 percent of Gulf War veterans, 11 percent of veterans of the war in Afghanistan, and 20 percent of Iraqi war veterans suffer from PTSD. Yet, the good men and women who serve our country are not the only ones at risk of developing PTSD. In fact, anyone exposed to a trauma—whether physical or psychological, whether distinct or ongoing—can develop this debilitating and life-altering condition. Little boys who grow up in homes where punches are thrown, little girls who suffer the incestuous reach of some older relative, teens who live and go to school in neighborhoods that are battlegrounds for drugs and gangs, and grown women caught in relationships that demean or batter them, all face the threat of this destructive condition. Unfortunately, in so many of these settings, there is a culture of silence that keeps people in a state of helplessness and isolation. Friends who witness abuse don't say anything. Teachers don't ask enough questions of their students. Family members don't talk about the terrible things they have experienced. Individuals who have PTSD need extensive and ongoing support to heal themselves and to reclaim their voices and their lives, but as long as they are wrapped in a web of silence—of embarrassment or shame—they cannot gain access to the very help and support they need. I often wonder how my own life might have been different if I hadn't waited so long to reach out and get help. How much less compounded would my PTSD have been? What kind of meaningful relationships with others might I have been capable of experiencing? How much pain and self-destruction might I have been spared?

I have written this book to break the spell of silence cast in my own family around the issues that led me to develop PTSD as a boy of eight; I also hope to help break the spell of silence we still face in our culture at large regarding PTSD or mental illness in general. To break the spell for myself that mental challenges of any type do not equate to being gay. Many years after my military service, I chose to safely experiment in gender balanced sexuality workshops,… mostly. During such exercises as hugging naked men and women,… I determined for myself,… that my sexual interests are geared toward women. Although psychological disorders like depression and anxiety have become more and more acknowledged in the mainstream culture, with nightly commercials on antidepressants gracing the television waves and numerous popular nonfiction books appearing on shelves in which authors admit to seeing a therapist for their grey moods or their neuroses, PTSD has remained relatively unexplored in the mainstream consciousness, other than its association with the military realm. Even then, the discussion remains a fairly narrow one, in which numbers of soldiers with the disorder are cited in an impersonal way.

This book tells the story of my own journey to healing with PTSD. It starts at the beginning, with the traumatic event in my childhood that caused me to develop the disorder, because every case of PTSD starts somewhere, whether due to a wartime battle, a natural disaster, a rape, an assault, or threats of death and violence to oneself or others. The book then traces my scary ride into darkness, from the early days at school when I couldn't concentrate in the classroom because of all the mental confusion in my mind, to the morning after I was voyeuristically peeped on,…possibly through the one inch gap in the closed stall door,…by a white military peer,…whom then went a step further by snitching on me for privately masturbating in a closed bathroom stall,…while at technical school training. This unknown individuals' choice of behavior,... and,... those individual men and women that blatantly chose to join in on what was a humiliating form of debauchery directed at me daily,... committed a horrible act. Additionally,... their repeated conscious choice of behavior was a psychologically violent attack and violation of my sovereign sexuality. At best,... and by definition,... what I experienced was sexual harassment / trauma committed by men,... and women. The hair on the back of my neck raised as I heard those words and my heartbeat raced upward in terror. That physical reaction toward verbal comments, laughter, loud sounds, and eventually even quiet sounds was normal for me, as my story will reveal, and is commonplace among those with PTSD.

By describing in this book my own reaction to the world around me—as well as by depicting my downward spiral from bad to worse, well beyond the night that I tried to commit suicide to the day 14 years later when the sound of my own stomach gurgling triggered me into a full-on attack of PTSD, I hope to give insight to those who know or love someone with PTSD regarding what individuals with this disorder face: the mental static and near-constant internal chaos, the deep-in-your-bones fear and paralysis, the isolating darkness and chains of silence. I also hope to give those with PTSD the courage to tell their stories. Most important, I hope that individuals in the current throes of battling the disorder who discover this book will recognize what might be going on inside of them and find the strength to reach out for the help they need to heal and rebuild their lives after experiencing the destruction that PTSD can wreak on one's love life, one's career, and one's family and home life.

My story ends with possibility, and it is my strongest wish in this book to share that real possibility of healing with those affected by PTSD who are currently feeling hopeless. Several years after I started to suspect that I had PTSD—and many years after the VA doctors had wrongly labeled me as schizophrenic—I learned of a treatment called EMDR, eye movement desensitization treatment and reprocessing. This procedure, which involves discussing the original traumatic event while using your eyes to follow a therapist's finger or pen movements, sounds almost absurd. In fact, when the procedure was first introduced by Francine Shapiro in the late 1980s, most psychologists and psychiatrists were skeptics. But the science now shows that EMDR is very effective,[11] as it helps the brain properly process the past trauma and forge new neuronal connections that lead to drastically improved mental health. In fact, EMDR is considered so effective that it was categorized in 2004 as "'strongly recommended' for the treatment of trauma" by the Veteran's Administration, which spends $4 billion treating approximately 200,000 veterans each year.[2,3]

After years of unrelenting pain, confusion, and frustration, EMDR changed my life; this change occurred, amazingly, within a relatively short time. During six months of regular EMDR treatment, one by one, several of the symptoms of my posttraumatic stress disorder began to decrease in frequency—the adrenaline rushes, the fast heart beat, the terrible night sweats and flashbacks, the hyper-vigilance. Now that my PTSD is in remission, I face the possibility of being able to rebuild my life as I choose. I still encounter daily struggles to feel emotions fully, to trust people, and to move past the negative messages of the verbal abuse I suffered as a child at the hands of my father, but the here-and-now physical symptoms of PTSD, which were triggered by simple sounds throughout the day, have begun to let me be. At one point in my life, I thought I wouldn't make it past the age of forty, sure that after years of suffering through exhaustive and repetitive PTSD-related adrenaline attacks, my body would break down and die of a heart attack. Today, at 45, I am living proof that people can begin to recover from PTSD and experience "normal" life like I am now doing—like enjoying steamed collard greens from my garden or hauling rocks around my yard to shape out some handsome landscaping instead of launching into full PTSD mode every time a car drives by the house or a thunder storm rolls in. I consider each day that I walk this earth to be a bonus. After all my years of suffering, I am thankful to be alive to tell my story, and I look forward to the possibility of bringing hope and understanding to your life or someone you know.

---

[1] American Psychiatric Association. (2004). Practice Guideline for the Treatment of Patients with Acute Stress Disorder and Post-traumatic Stress Disorder. Arlington, VA: American Psychiatric Association Practice Guidelines.

[2] Department of Veterans Affairs and Department of Defense. (2004). VA/ DoD Clinical Practice Guideline for the Management of Post-Traumatic Stress. Washington, DC.

[3] Wilson, D., & Barglow, P. (2009). PTSD Has Unreliable Diagnostic Criteria. Psychiatric Times, 26(7).

Chapter 1

The Incident

When I was eight years old, a gun went off, and I lost my voice. In that moment after my father pulled the trigger, my soul lifted off the ground. One half an inch, that's all it jumped,... 1.27 centimeters. But when my soul came back down and re-entered my body, that voice of mine didn't come back down with it. Several decades later I would realize that some part of me deep inside had died that summer day in 1972. To the casual observer, my "death" was just as silent and invisible as that of my voice; in fact, I never cried about the incident until I was in my mid-30's. Ever heard a dead man talk? Well, neither had I until I looked in the mirror. I was 41 years old in a therapy session when I finally acknowledged, by stopping myself in mid-sentence, about to say once more that "no one got hurt when the gun fired." Instead, I paused and looked at my therapist, my mouth hanging open with a sudden sense of discovery and said in a whispery voice, "I got hurt....That's why I've been having all these problems.... that's why I've been in therapy so much. I got hurt." My eyes, which had been widely fixed in a catatonic-like gaze, welled up with the tears of my revelation. Feelings of shame and guilt swirled confusingly through my mind. How could I accuse my parents who obviously loved me? And how could I let all that emotion show when I was sitting in full view of another man? Would my therapist, Russell, look down on me? Russell maintained his composure so as not to rob me of my self-discovery in that moment; then, some of his pleasure slipped through his professionalism, in the form of a slight lip-pursing that stopped just short of the beginning of a full-scale smile. I can only assume that he had long since figured out that I had gotten hurt during the domestic violence between my parents in which case he surely must have been pleased by the fact that I finally had realized and said it. But, at the time, I felt uncomfortable revealing this vulnerable part of myself in front of him. I felt a strong sense of accomplishment in that moment even though I didn't know what to do with the feeling. Yet, I also felt confused about my revelation that my parents had hurt me so profoundly, even if they had done so unintentionally. Their desire to kill each other was purposeful—that, I could not deny; their regard for the 8-year-old child was undetectable if not outright void. What happened to my voice on that summer day when the bullet of my father's gun tore through the floor? Where did that voice of mine go? Did it float up and get stuck in a tree, like a sad balloon with so much possibility that just became tangled and torn in the branches, then deflated and defeated, a rubber remnant waving in the wind, lost, forgotten? In a family where there was so much fussing and fighting and I was the youngest, my voice was all I had: the voice to say, "These greens taste terrible," or "I feel sad," or "Can I tell you something?" like when my youngest sister Landy and 5th youngest sister Francine took me to the shoe store in downtown Knoxville in 1971, and I said, simply, "These shoes hurt my feet." They bought those shoes for me anyway because Dad said I had to have a new pair and my sisters sure as hell weren't gonna go against him. Then Dad got mad at me for not wearing them even though they hurt. I was both visible and invisible to him: he could always see the parts of me that needed fixing and correcting, but all that was good in me—or in need of love—drifted right past his gaze. Even then, with those too-small shoes, things were still okay, though. Maybe I had to wear those shoes, maybe my feet hurt when I walked in them, maybe I got blisters, maybe I was upset at my dad or my sisters—but I still had my voice, a voice to say what was bothering me or to ask for what I wanted, and that was something. Like the day I was at my older cousin Corey's house in South Carolina and I asked, "Can I have some more plums?" I must have been only three or four years old then and Mom would oftentimes refer to that event as I grew up in Knoxville. That plum tree in cousin Corey's yard was so beautiful and those plums tasted so juicy so that I never even thought two times about whether I could ask my cousin for some more plums. The world was still mine back then. It was full of promise and possibility. The world was full of plums waiting to be picked and eaten.

When I was stationed at an Air Force base years later, in 1986, I attended a family reunion in Columbia and stepped on that same front porch that I had sat on nineteen years earlier; cousin Corey was in her 80's or 90's by then, and she remembered me and the story about asking for more plums. As a matter of fact, she brought up the subject! But I was in full PTSD mode that day and couldn't humor an old woman her fond remembrances. I couldn't chuckle or grin. I couldn't collect that happy memory out of her still-standing plum tree—because I was too busy feeling humiliated by my tense body and sweaty palms—the near constant state of PTSD torment that I unknowingly carried around with me everywhere. Of course, cousin Corey, cousin Estelle, and the others at the formal dinner that night couldn't possibly have known how twisted up my insides really were, but I was so knotted up with the hot fear and pounding heart of my PTSD that I spent all evening worrying they would figure me out. And so it was with PTSD: I was buried not just under that sense of fear that I was about to be attacked by some nebulous and terrible thing, but all that fear was overloaded with worry about what others might think of me, topped with my embarrassment and shame. Maybe that is why I couldn't speak. Maybe that is why I couldn't tell my family I needed their help: because of all that embarrassment and shame. Of course, I have to ask—would it have even mattered if I had asked? If I had reached out to them, I don't think they would have known what to do. My parents couldn't talk to each other in a civil sentence. Helping me climb out of the black hole of my madness was surely beyond their grasp. Not that all my memories of my parents were bad. When I was a kid, my father taught me how to garden while we lived in the house on Ashland Avenue. In the space of all that earth and sky and quiet, he would teach me how to sprinkle bone meal into the soil so the tomato plants didn't get blossom-end rot. He would dig the holes and let me fill them. I would lay the roots of the tomato plants into the soil and discover what it felt like to foster a small piece of life. There are a few precious memories of my mother that I carry too. Like the days before I was old enough to go to school and I walked around the neighborhood with Mom, and no one or nothing else was with us—no yelling daddy, no hickory-handled butcher knife, no nickel-plated, semiautomatic hand gun. We walked the streets of our old neighborhood on Bethel street, to the houses they were tearing down across the way so they could build some affordable housing. I stood fascinated while those life-sized Tonka trucks—those yellow bulldozers and backhoes—shoveled and rearranged broken rock and dirt. Who might I have become if that was all my young life had been made of—walks around the neighborhood with Mom and quiet moments tending the garden with Dad? What kind of man might I have grown into? Maybe I would have retired from the Air Force as a three-star general. Maybe I would have graduated Suma Cum Laude from Harvard. Maybe I would have married and had children, been able to go back to Knoxville for family holidays, or kept a job beyond my 38th birthday. That would have been something. What measure of my life can I take when I can almost see who I *might* have been? Does a boy's desire for picking plums count for something? Was my delight in the silver birds that cut through the sky above my childhood home as they left the nearby airport enough to say my life was worth it? I'll never know what my life might have been without all that fussing and fighting, without the daily callouts by my father who seemed to believe I could never do anything right—because a couple of years after the plum tree and the walks around the neighborhood, a gun went off in my living room just two feet from the piano and from my mom and me and all that green furniture and Landy, balled up on the couch hyperventilating from trying not to cry. My father's arm jerked with that shiny silver gun, his hands unmistakably gripping the pearl inlaid handle, and a bullet exploded through the hardwood floor one foot from my own feet, maybe two from my ranting and crying mother. In that moment, the world cracked open and my soul jumped half an inch. In the second that my father fired that gun, the bullet that released didn't just shoot through the floor, it tore through me first, invisibly shredding my insides, fraying my brain, and reprogramming the way I would think and feel and speak (or not speak) from that day forward. An assault took place on my nervous system that would silently and insidiously rob me of emotional peace for the next thirty-three years of my life. And my voice? Well it flew out of me that day and disappeared, making like it might never come back. Here's how it all went down.

"LANDY," my dad boomed. "Get over there and sit on the couch. I told you to stop crying!" Landy, with tears in her eyes, hesitantly moved over to the green couch that was situated lengthwise in front of the living room picture window. Like a frightened mouse she held herself tight with arms crossed as she tried to hold back her tears in an attempt to obey Dad's order to stop crying (even though crying was the natural and sane thing for Landy to be doing). I on the other hand continued standing within two feet of my screaming parents with dry eyes and bone-chilling tension in my body, like it was a winter's day and my body needed to shiver to generate heat. My throat was dry, too, and I was afraid to swallow for fear of making any kind of sound that might cause me to get into trouble with Dad like my sister had. He never ordered me to the couch. So I stood in the doorway between the bedroom and living room, next to the upright piano to my left and the consol stereo to my right with the front door just beyond the stereo by a few feet. Why I never ran out the door I will never know… fear is one good reason, I imagine; confusion is another. From the doorway where I stood looking into our small living room, I could still hear Landys' terrible sobs, the gasps and sucking-in sounds that should have come because she had fallen off her lime green Mohawk bike with that black and green banana seat and skinned her knee. Not because her Daddy was holding a gun (semi-automatic, pearl handle, nickel plated, 25 caliber) and Mama was wielding a well-worn butcher knife (blackened steel, hickory handle with brass rivets) in addition to both parents screaming so loud that surely the neighbors could have heard the explosive drama playing out like an old-time radio show! You know the kind—Alfred Hitchcock, for example—one of the all-time masters of horror and suspense without the use of blood and gore. Little did I know that Hitchcock-like horror would soon start haunting me and I would have to live with it for 33 more years after witnessing a real life drama.

"Howard!" my 5'5" mother roared wildly at my dad (who was my namesake), with every strand of her medium-length, black, coarse hair (which she rolled every night with small plastic-clasped foam-filled hair-rollers) amazingly still in place. She waved that solid steel butcher knife, frantically in the air, with its 12-inch blade and a spine at least a quarter inch thick, so blackened with age that it must have been at least twenty years old if it was a day at that time. Back then knives were made like cars—heavy and with lots of basic steel. Dad—all towering six-foot-two-inches of him—yelled back at her, the small silvery-looking gun wildly moving around as he held onto it and gestured. Then, in a fit of anger at my Mom's words, my dad's arm jerked slightly forward at an angle, but mostly downward. He shot the gun—and a bullet ripped through the hardwood floor not more than one foot in front of me and to my left, leaving a mark that was never talked about by anyone including me until I was about 35 years old in a therapy session. That's how we did it in my family. Mom and dad would go crazy with fights every day, though not with weapons each time, and the house, full with people, would empty itself, like an animal that had gotten sick. My nieces and nephews would be led out the door, and my older siblings would close that door right behind them, leaving my sister Landy and me to all the yelling, ranting and raving, the sometimes hitting—to the hickory-handled butcher knife and the nickel-plated gun. When the fighting was through, none of us ever talked about it—not my neighbors, not my parents, not my sisters, not me. I was trapped in the silence, an unlucky feather of a kid caught in a sick web that I call the "pretend game." And that web just kept on growing, just kept on wrapping itself more and more around me like a cocoon until I could hardly see. One day, I would break out of that cocoon, though, and become my own butterfly, wings a little wrinkled and folded, trouble flying often, but some semblance of the creature I was supposed to be. Of course, that one day was still long, long into my future. Until then, I was stuck with the splinters of a bullet that had just ripped through my world—and riddled my body with PTS. In my case, it was a gunshot that fractured my brain and frayed my nervous system. If I had been a child soldier in Rwanda, my brain might have gotten fried by my pulling the trigger on my enemy. If I had lived on a tropical island far away, maybe a tsunami washing my mother away would have broken me. If I had served in Vietnam, witnessing a rape or experiencing torture could have done it. PTS always starts with some kind of trauma. But I was Howard Lovely, Jr., resident of Ashland Avenue in Knoxville, Tennessee, and I lived with two parents who screamed at each other every day for one reason or another, whose mom one day pulled out a butcher knife and whose dad fired his gun one foot from his wife and son. For me, the gun shot is what did it, but it could have been something else, something bad enough to make me know, in my bones, that I or someone I loved was about to die.

Chapter 2

The Fallout

The green of the school chalkboard stretched endlessly before me as I sat at my desk just a few yards away, with my eyes frozen on the surface as three of my fellow students scrambled to dissect sentences. Subject. Verb. Direct object. They would draw a slanted line underneath each word in question and then write its descriptive name. I could hear every word that my teacher was saying at the time; I could see all the movement of my classmates. Yet my body was tense—wound tight as an old alarm clock—and my mind seemed to be frozen in a way that I was aware of but could not break free of—like when one is having a dream of being chased and trying to wake up from sleep but not being able to exercise enough control to snap one's body into wakefulness. I had that feeling just then in the classroom, of being asleep and awake at the same time, of watching the scene unfold before me as if from an REM state. "Stop day dreaming Howard!!!" My teacher yelled suddenly, and humiliation for being singled out in the class radiated throughout my body. I couldn't control my daze any more than I could control my father's firing that gun. And I sure couldn't explain what was going on to my teacher because I hardly understood things myself. I told her I had heard everything, but she didn't believe me: probably because I could not repeat a single world of what I had heard. In that moment,… I should have told her that my body felt like maggots were crawling all around in and on me. That strange trance-like state I faced in the classroom back then would persist for nearly four decades. It would continue to randomly occur even while I was driving or doing anything for that matter. What caused my brain to malfunction in that way? Maybe it was all that sporadic chaos in my head, the chipped bits of conversation, the little shards of anger, the ragged rants of my mother, the razor-sharp commands of my father, the predictable tide of self-hatred that I always felt when my father said to me: "You can't do anything without Dad's help." Those words still move around in my mind to this very day,… like little maggots eating away at my brain. Did my dad really think I was that worthless? Did he truly want me to be that helpless? Was his cutting me down all the time the only way he could figure out how to pump himself up, sucking air out of any room where I or another member of his family stood, so he wouldn't deflate into nothingness? Dad was intelligent, skilled, and accomplished; Dad took care of his family. When he wasn't putting my six older sisters and me through all that junk, he was a kind and loving father. But dad must have had a story that drowned his kindness and sent cruelty occasionally floating to the top. Dad had grown up among the Jim Crow laws of the South, which told him to sit in the back, to eat over there, not to drink at that fountain, to work at only certain jobs in the military (supply Sergeant First Class), and to save that water fountain and bathroom for the White folks. Dad & Mom had no civil-rights or voting rights until after I was born in 1964 & 65 respectively. Dad was programmed by mainstream society to believe that he was not good enough, that regardless of whatever he accomplished, he would always be considered less than. I suspected that he responded to all the putdowns by struggling to build himself up anyway that he could. Out in the world, dad was a Black man who had surely suffered all manner of discrimination and humiliation (though those stories were locked up deep inside of him like little worms eating away at his goodness). At our house, though, dad could be eminent ruler of the domain—and that's who he chose to be. The dictator. "Howard? Howard?!" My teacher raised her voice, trying to get my attention and, by doing so, unwittingly calling me back to the classroom in a more present emotional state. "What's the answer to the problem?" Her moving lips told me that I was supposed to be saying something in return, but my own mouth wouldn't budge. I just sat at my desk frightened, physically frozen, emotionally confused and all wrapped up in my web. I was alone in a room full of people. "Howard? Did you hear me?" she asked again, bending over and squinting her eyes at me, studying my face for some sign of understanding. Little did My teacher know that it was she who needed to understand me, just as much as she wanted me to understand the grammar lesson that she was teaching. My teacher (and many other teachers) misdiagnosed my behavior as being simply "day dreaming." I sometimes wonder how might things have been different if she had really known what was going on behind my glassy eyes?

After the gun shot, I started waking in the middle of the night and every morning with bed sheets so wet I might as well have pissed them. The sheets were soaked with sweat so putrid, not in scent but in outright emotional terribleness, that they might as well have been an ocean ready to swallow me. Those bad dreams would chase me for years. Once I had witnessed my own mortality through the crackle of my father's gunshot—the way my life could be snatched from me without hesitation or justification or verification—death seemed to lurk around every corner. My life's sole purpose was to evade it, escape it, out run it. Maybe my life would have been different if all that fright and terror could have just stayed hidden in my room, under the cloak of darkness while I fought sleep. Maybe if I could have just contained my desperate fear to the nighttime, I could have managed to live during the daytime—to trust other people enough to make real friends, to stand up for myself when a few jerks in the Service teased me, to not think continually about killing myself to end all the pain, to force the doctors at the VA to see that they weren't helping me and I needed a different medical treatment. Maybe I would have been able to speak to My teacher when she commanded me to do so. But my PTSD (though I didn't know it by that name yet) was relentless. It chased me not just through nighttime, but through all the daytime hours too—through every classroom and down every street and alley. It found me standing in the shower or sitting at the kitchen table. Its pursuit was constant. Every time a car backfired or a kid yelled to another on a bicycle or a teacher yelled at me while I stood frozen at the chalkboard, my body rushed into defense mode, ready to fight or ready to flee, with my head thinking, *save yourself* and my body responding physiologically.

At the time, I didn't know what was happening to me. I was so young, I hardly knew normal from not, right side up from down. But years later, I began to see that, once activated, PTSD can slowly destroy a person's life, responsibility by responsibility, relationship by relationship, job opportunity by job opportunity. How could I as a boy maintain a friendship when I was unable to trust even my own body, which seemed to constantly betray and contradict itself? How could I as a man report for duty when all day long, each unexpected sound that broke the silence sent my whole body tingling into reaction with uncontrolled adrenaline? How could I as a man get a woman to love me when I was terrified to sit in a restaurant by myself, let alone with a lady dining by my side? How could I have known as an individual, the difference between my imagination and reality when my body sees rain clouds everywhere and keeps opening the umbrella? After the gun shot, my brain was by all manner of speaking severed in two. The sensory input taken in by my right brain stopped being moderated by my more logical left brain, and as a result I was no longer able to completely reason all that input into its proper place. *That's just the sound of someone's name being called over a loud-speaker*, I should have been able to think. *That's just the noise of a rivet gun running, as my coworker fixes an airplane.* But after the trauma, I lost the ability to make rational sense of my minute-by-minute environment, and those right-brain thoughts had my body firing all the time to protect it from the sensory assaults I encountered throughout the day. How long can a person continuously live in defense mode, shivering under the cover of darkness, ready to pounce if found? For how many years can a person hold up a heavy shield while running backwards? In my case, the answer turned out to be more than three decades.

Chapter 3

Trying to Escape

Tink. Tink. Tink My Dad clinked some metal as he fiddled with the pipes. I was just out of high school by then and we were doing one of our home improvement projects. This time it was the bathtub.

"Hand me the smaller wrench", my Dad said calmly, while puffing on a cigarette held off to the side of his mouth. The smoke burned my eyes but I always tolerated Mom and Dad's smoke, both literally and figuratively.

From my crouched position between the sink and toilet, I located the smaller rusty pipe – wrench on the floor. The downstairs bathroom that we were working in was very small,… maybe 5' X 10' at best,… which made for a very cramped working space. Though as a kid,…I didn't mind because moments like these were relatively easy,…and comprised of no arguing,…no yelling,…just a me and Dad,…turning something old into something new again. I thought to myself,… "If I'm lucky,… things will stay quiet like this",… "Dad will not start complaining to me about Mom as usual",… making me his own personal therapist,… Mom did the same too. I always felt an odd sense of loyalty confliction in those emotionally abusive moments; nevertheless, I simply listened to Dad or Mom because that was damn well all I could do. I was just a kid who did not want to upset my parents,… I wanted to please them. I was not going to choose sides because I looked up to and valued both of my parents. However,… as an adult,… I now understand that looking back on those moments is a mental exercise that reveals a potent mixture of disgust, limited understanding, and inadvertent twisted psychological education.

As my Dad leaned inward toward the pipe with the wrench he used to loosen something, I heard more clinking metal from the kitchen. It was Mom, slamming down pots. Bang!... Bang!... Bang! She was angry about something Dad said to her earlier.

"You want me to put all this meat in the freezer?!" She yelled grumpily from the kitchen, toward my Father. "Why can't we have a brick house like aunt Margarets'?!" she added in a low voice.

My Dad appeared to be focusing on the plumbing, but I knew he had heard Mom's complaints. They were like rusty barbs in his brain. I heard every one of them also and unfortunately felt as though they were directed at me sometimes. I thought to myself,... "here I am working on fixing our house with Dad,...and in so many words,... Mom is saying the house still isn't good enough". An odd sense of shame and unworthiness bubbled up in me,... but I didn't understand the psychological programming that my Mother was inadvertently doing to me back then,... but I sure felt it. "Pass me a beer Junior.",... my Dad said.

Minutes went by as I did what I always did,.... I pretended that everything would be OK. I passed the half empty can to my Dad and watched him down the entire contents. A loud,...deep belch escaped his mouth and collided with the high-pitched sound of the aluminum can being placed on the floor,... where it instantly became an impromptu ashtray.

"Yo Mama don't know nothing",... Dad complained. Now I knew for sure that Dad had heard every word Mama had been mumbling previously,... but I did what I always did: remained tense but silent, gazed at Dad and listened. I always felt so awkward in those moments (those moments of which there were just too many to count).

As an adult I realized that in part I was inadvertently and inappropriately being used as a quasi-therapist in moments like that.

"I ain't putting that meat away!",... my Mother screamed louder from the kitchen.

I was having trouble finding a small screw that Dad needed to secure a bracket to the pipes under the tub. I leaned my head in deep, and used my bare hand to burrow a little tunnel through all the tools,...until my fingers hit bottom. "I found it",... I said to my Dad.

"God Damn you, I'm sick and tired of you treating me this way!",... My Mothers' voice billowed toward the bathroom in a hurry as her footsteps creaked loudly in the hallway in a flash coming ever closer. I looked up and there she was,…lunging toward her Husband,… my Father,… with that damn well-used butcher knife! I was closer to the door than my Dad and Mom nearly stabbed me in the left side of my neck as I turned to my right,… reacting due to my peripheral vision.

Holy shit! I thought.

That knife went flying right past my jugular,… one more inch to the left and she would have stabbed me. Two feet more in a forward direction,… and she would have gotten Dad in the back!

Damn it!

Not this shit again,… I thought to myself.

"I'm so tired of you treating me this way!" My Mom muttered along with tears and other incoherently screamed words, while waving the knife wildly through the air.

"What the hell you doing?!" My Dad yelled while turning and jumping to his feet fast. "You never gonna live to see the end of this day!" I jumped to my feet in perfect lockstep with my Dad as all three of us moved in some sick, nearly choreographed unison,… I in the middle,…while switching my gaze of horror from front to rear in an effort to keep track of both parents' movements.

As an adult Male in my early 40's,… I finally realized that in that moment,…NO one was thinking of me,… the teen-aged child. Neither of the parents were thinking of their Sons' safety and I was care-taking both parents rather than myself.

That's how we rolled at my house,… it was an explosive zero-to-sixty,…a living hell for sure and I couldn't do a damn thing about it as a kid.

I'm sure it's a very saddening spectacle of a story to hear about the antics of parents who trampled all over their child,… mentally and physically.

My Father reached toward my Mother to grab her wrist but she slipped away and started running back down the hallway.

Dad raced after her angrily,… but I was tangled between them and mentally trying to figure out exactly what was going on. "Weren't we just fixing the bathtub?!",… I thought to myself.

Dad and I entered the kitchen as Mom braced her back against the stove. My Dad kept leaping toward Mom, but I was big enough now that

I was able to block Dad by moving my body into Dad's way,... right, left, right. I didn't know how long I could keep all this up.

"What you doin coming at me with a knife?!" My dad yelled at Mom.

"Just what the hell do you think you're doin?!".

"You know exactly what I'm doing!",... I'm tired of you treatin me this way!",... "You always saying such mean things to me!".

That did it. Dad thrust his body as hard as he could past me to get at Mom,... but I "saw" it coming and threw my body back at Dad even harder. I was nearly twenty,... growing into a Man of my own. Mom was so much smaller than dad. Her words could bite,... but his hits were too strong.

"Junior!",... Howard's Father yelled,... while getting his arms underneath my arm-pits and around the back of my neck,... with his fingers locking me into a head-lock so that I stood with my upper body immobilized. So now I stood in an emasculating and humiliating position right in front of my Mother and at the hands of my Father. "That's enough out of you!",... Dad said to Mom while still tied up with me. Damn it!,... he had gotten a hold of me. Why did Dad always have to win? Why couldn't I beat him for once? Then I thought,... "at least Dad's not hittin Mom while I'm in a head-lock". This last thought would prove to be an error on my part because I physically relaxed at the thought of Mom's temporary safety, Dad realized I was not trying to harm him or resist and thus released me,... but everything between Him and Mom started up again...

The bafflement of that moment stays with me today.

As I write this,.... My emotions have immediately taken a very *dark* turn as the life seems to drain out of me,... my facial skin appears to have shriveled and taken on a dry un-taut look,... much like a deceased person would look.

I often retrospectively wonder what kind of value my parents placed on my life when one of them was willing to nearly slash my throat and the other was willing to risk snapping my neck?!

All this took place within a matter of five minutes or so of heated anger over relatively nothing.

To this very day,... I feel searing pain in my chest when I recount this single event among many,... as if the representation of the idea of "Love" juxtaposed with the heart,… has been burnt,… seared with a hot *sword* of confusion placed squarely through my chest that day,… long ago in 1984.

As I write about this event,… my breathing skips and heart appears to stop beating. I feel like a talking *dead* Man. My spirit has long since *died*.

I often feel as if my neck,… if only in my mind,… had been metaphorically slashed & snapped by my parents like some sick tag-team,… and no one saw the *blood* or heard the *snap* due to the yelling back and forth.

It gives me the chills so say the least.

I remember my blood rushing to my face and I gasped for oxygen,… my Mother yelled "You don't know how to care for no one",… "why you always putting me down?" she said,… with tears soaking her cheeks.

I moved back toward the kitchen table while Dad and Mom started shoving and hitting each other. I watched those two fools push and holler at each other with no one else there to see it but me. No neighbors, no sisters, not even sister Landy who had gone off to college by then to escape the *house-of-hell*.

I was all alone in that living hell,… with those two Sam-Walking-Fools trying to kill each other.

"Get your hands off me!",… my Mother screamed at Dad,… while attempting to shake him loose. Having recovered my balance,… I rushed in and got an arm around Mom and hurried her toward the front door with my Dad just steps behind me.

"Go-on,… Mom,… get out of here",… I told her as I opened the front screen door and helped her down the stairs. "You got to get out of here". "Go call Aunt Mattie". I stood there internally conflicted as I watched my Mom cross the lawn and head toward the neighbor's house. She knocked and my neighbor's head popped out the door long enough to shake her head yes, as she scanned our front porch with angry eyes. Her eyes fell on me,… and I felt guilt deep within myself. There was no time for pity,… the neighbor just pulled my Mom into her house and closed the door.

"They're nuts…", I thought to myself as I stared at the closed door and thought about Mom & Dad. "Them two fools are absolutely nuts". As I write of this incidence I wonder: "How many times in the course of my life had they fought so hard that my Mother had to run?",… additionally,…

"How many more times in the course of all seven of their childrens' lives had they clawed and taken swipes at each other?".

I took a deep breath and walked inside the house. My blood was pounding in my ears and I went to sit down on the green couch to see if I could calm down. My Father was still in the house,… I knew because I could hear him banging things around in the kitchen. Then it got quiet and I thought I heard him walking down the hallway toward the bathroom. I continued to sit there on that old green couch,… breathing and thinking back to an earlier event. It was the same couch I had seen my youngest sister curl up on ten years earlier,… a ball of hysterics as my Father readied to kill my Mother with a gun. Sister Landy had known to instinctively cry back then,… without her even thinking about it those tears began to flow. They rushed a river out from inside her so that all that seeming hatred between our parents,… all that terror they weaved through our home environment,… did not get stick inside her,…. at least not like I now know that it had gotten stuck in me for all these years.

As I present day think about what had happened back then,… when that gun-shot ripped through the house in 1972,… the anger and terror sliced down the middle of my brain and got trapped there,… where it has painfully remained for 41 years. I didn't know how to cry it out,… maybe because I was a boy in a male dominated culture that trained me not to cry,… maybe because I was too young,… maybe because I was so stunned that all the wind had been frightened out of me and there was no oxygen left to fuel the outburst that should have naturally come forth.

As an older Man,… I currently wonder that if I had been culturally allowed to cry,… would my mental-well-being / life have been different?…. I wonder if my brain would have processed the events in such a way that would have allowed me to be free from years of mental torment that I eventually experienced.

While sitting on that couch I was awakened from my moment of remembrance by the sound of my Dad down the hallway. I heard the faucet in the bathroom. The sound of running water vibrated through my body suddenly. I scanned the ceiling,… resisting the urge to flee,… I searched for a crack or anything to focus my attention on. My skin prickled while the blood raced in my veins and I silently wanted *"it"* to stop.

From the bathroom I heard my Dad's voice belt in a low tone,… "Junior!",… " C-mon back in here",… "Let's finish the job".

I thought to myself,… "What?,… Fix the bathtub?" I stood up from my seated position on the old green couch and walked dutifully but with conflicted loyalty,… down the hallway.

I headed in the direction of my Dad but simultaneously chose a silent defiant stance. Dad had been on me for many months about going to college. I did not want to attend college but enough was enough at this point. Life at college couldn't be any worse than here,… and I desperately had to get out of that hell-pit. I knew that I needed to enroll as soon as possible because my parents were figuratively driving me crazy. Little did I know that they were literally driving me "crazy".

I arrived into the bathroom where my Father promptly ordered in an angry low toned voice,… "Go get me a beer!".

"Yo Mama makes me sick",… Dad grumbled to me with a low tone of disgust and down cast eyes.

I was the one feeling sick with being thrust into the role of therapist for the "millionth" time. I went and got Dads' beer from the refrigerator and passed it to him while waiting for his next command.

Zero-To-Sixty,… to zero emotion.

That's how we did things in our house.

As if none of the previous accounting of events had ever happened.

We just picked up wherever we had left off,… like we had finished eating a bag of potato chips and drank a soda,… as if the butcher knife was still in the drawer,… and my Mom was in the kitchen bagging 100 pounds of meat for freezing.

In the span of about an hour,… I emotionally and physically took-care of both parents, was nearly killed by both parents and did nothing for myself accept stuff my feelings deep inside myself.

Of the three individuals present that day,… no one thought of me,… including me.

Chapter 4

Never Again

Several months later I enrolled in school at Walters' State Community College located in Morristown, 30 miles from home, where I and my roommate would stuff our freezer full of fresh chicken seconds from the outlet store on Magnolia avenue and our cupboards with plenty of canned goods and Jiffy-Mix boxes of cornbread mix, for only a hundred dollars split between us each month. Over break, I went home to visit with my family. As I was receiving a check from my dad to pay for the next quarter, my dad said the usual: "You can't do anything without your dad's help". I smiled awkwardly,… as if at a joke that was not funny. I did as I always did,… just taking my dad's verbal abuse,… and accepted the check from him reluctantly because it came laden with a heavy feeling of guilt, shame and emasculation. These words were not even in my vocabulary back then,… yet the sensory feeling was rooted deep in my gut and unmistakable. Something clicked in my head once more: "You will never say that to me again",…. I thought angrily to myself while still gazing at my Father's eyes and holding that awkward smile. When I returned to school, I walked the tuition check over to the bursar's office to pay for the next quarter and then went directly to take the test needed to enlist in the military. I had decided that this was going to be my last quarter at school. I didn't tell my father that I had joined the Air Force until two weeks before basic training, and my dad was infuriated when he found out. My Dad yelled at me in front of my Mother as if I was an eight year old child. I was a young Man of 21 years now but it seemed as though my Father was dead set on emasculating me into submission for some reason unknown to me at that time. My Father seemed hell-bent on not allowing me to grow into an independent and confident Man. My Father was a short-sighted idiot like that and my Mother stood by silently and never came to my defense. I have long since deeply resented my now 85 year old Mother and deceased Father. In retrospect,... I struggle to reconcile the behavior of my parents,... what kind of parents,... especially a Dad,... would choose to raise a "dependent-panty-waste" for a Son? Then send him out into the world.

Was my Father possibly functioning from a place of sickening fear and an ingrained morphed version of Jim-Crow South "law" that required a Black Man to be demeaningly subservient on demand,... to any White person including a White child?

My Father may have been still operating from this frame of reference to train me to survive. If this is the case in part,...my story may prove to be a devastatingly horrible example of how such human behavior as racism / bigotry and short-sightedness,... can be passed on generationally in a psychologically hidden form with profound and devastating consequences.

Anyway,...I had an insatiable desire to get as far away from my parents as possible and would eventually spend very little time visiting them once I left Knoxville, Tennessee.

While waiting to go to basic training, I worked at Levi Strauss pressing jeans. I caught the eye of a beautiful Black / Cherokee young woman (the same ethnicity as my grandmother), named "Z," who was sewing jeans across the room. We dated a few weeks until I left for basic training.

Nine years later,... my choice and early childhood experiences at the hands of my parents would prove to have profound consequences in the final conscious hours of my Father,...just before his death in January 1994.

Chapter 5

I'm Being Followed (by PTSD)

I left Knoxville, Tennessee, and flew to an Air Force Base for 8 weeks of basic training. It was the first plane I'd ever taken and I was excited. But once at training, which was hard as hell, I missed Z, who had sent me letters at Basic Training and many weeks later at Technical School. One night while at Technical School at an Air Force base in Illinois, I went into a bathroom stall to pleasure myself; after checking to be sure no one else was present, lost myself in the moment while thinking of "Z". But someone walked in and heard me. As I watched two white legs stop in front of my stall and then walk out, adrenaline flooded my system. my privacy had been violated and my body got triggered back to a similar emotional feeling like the moment when my dad fired the gun many years earlier nearly killing me. As I snuck out of the bathroom and heard laughter down the hall from guys telling jokes in the rec room, I was racing into full PTSD mode. I rushed to my dorm-room and sat on my bed, thinking, "What have I done?" The next day at breakfast, another Black airman, "B," cracked a joke as I walked by with my tray. "How're the wife and kids?" he asked me meanly. In front of at least a hundred of my fellow male and female military peers, I felt deeply humiliated and frozen with a generalized fear. As the group finished breakfast and fell into formation, B cracked another joke: "How's the baloney bopping going, Lovely?" The whole formation, at least three flights comprised of one hundred airmen and women, including the leadership (ropes), broke into a lawless uproar of laughter. I Could feel my body had frozen stiff as if I was paralyzed or a statue on display. I felt excruciating emotional & physical pain in that moment and hoped it didn't show outwardly as I remained at attention,… which must have served as an indicator of personal distress rather than duty,…under the horrible and obvious circumstances. One day later,… while in class,… one of the Staff Sergeant instructors J called me "wing-nut" in reference to the masturbation incident,… I was so shocked & horrified that this person of such rank and authority joined in on the humiliation campaign with unbridled alienating contempt, rather than mentor me as a Man or at the very least refrain from such a despicable and based behavior as a Non-Commissioned Officer. I was in such a mistrustful and dazed state of mind and did not understand my lack of violent reaction at that time,… emotional or physical,… that would have been warranted under the despicable circumstances,….I just simply endured the abuse like I had been trained to do,… by my abusive parents. I would later experience numerous situations in which the rank-and-file directly participated or stood idly by while I blatantly took blow after blow after blow for the entire five years ten months and some odd number of days & hours that I can recall at this time,… the actions of my "superiors" which amounted to dereliction of duty under the Uniform Code Of Military Justice (UCMJ),…in my mind. Many of the instructors that told off-color jokes of a sexual nature on occasion during class and I did my best to keep a straight face but from the corner of my eye I noticed many class mates stirring at me as an indication that I was the target of the joke. I could feel their piercing hypocritical Religious / Christian energy permeating my body intensely like a thousand knifes as my skin crawled beneath my clothing all during class. My eyes would well up with torturous tears that I dared not let loose for fear that they too would drown my in a tsunami of betrayal. As if I had never questioned myself under the oppressive scrutiny of my fathers' eyes and voice,… I began to question myself on every level of my existence in this world as I had obviously traded one hellish environment of betrayal,… in which I grew up,… for another comprised of treachery in green uniforms of the United States Air Force. Where was the allegiance of Airmen that the uniform was supposed to have represented? Where was the allegiance of Men, Masculinity and that sacred behavior that had long since been deemed base? Where was the Pledge of Allegiance that I was encouraged to recite in grade school along with all the other children with our hands placed over our hearts?

Where was the allegiance of Christianity of which most, if not all the individuals present at that time would have sworn to have held dear as a Religious faith,… including me? All these questions and more welled up in my eyes, heart, soul and mind. These questions could be summed up with one word,… betrayal. I betrayed myself in my choice of venue and was betrayed on the most profound levels by most individuals around my. As with my childhood home environment,…I once more,…was confronted with the idea that no place is *safe* and that Religious / Spiritual *beliefs* are just meaningless words unless they are lived daily,… via actions. My experiences during the middle 1980's were "sandwiched" between two major social events (global onset of HIV & firing of Joycelyn Elders). The HIV virus was just appearing to run rampant among Gay Men around 1979 - 1980 and there was still a great amount of fear swirling around anything sexually related. Of course mass hysteria grew faster than the HIV virus and even though heterosexuals masturbate also,… in my mind masturbation hypocritically got associated with being Gay,… apparently. This proved to be a very unfortunate, potently sick, social mixture for me when a private matter,…was taken public by one unknown White Man that chose to commit a lone act of betrayal among Men. Even the Surgeon General,… *Joycelyn Elders, MD,*…was fired /asked to resign her post,… for publicly advocating Masturbation as a [healthy private] sexual outlet in lieu of partnered sex. That took place during the Clinton Administration in the 1990's and almost a decade after my experience began. It was a sad social commentary to say the least. Of all the individuals that participated in the *campaign* to make me a social pariah,… and there were hundreds comprised of many different races, military rank and Religion,… no one ever seemed to question their own frenzied, perverted version, of un-invited and definitely unwanted voyeuristic sexual focus on me. My actions of private masturbation,… was well within parameters of healthy human sexual behavior since the beginning of time when Man discovered his Lingham. The actions of all those who harassed, taunted and engage in unrelenting voyeuristic focus on me,… in the context of an assumed educated and civilized society,…. gave clear indication of actions way out of bounds in terms of normal, healthy, rational social behavior,… especially considering the fact that all of it was rooted in destructive hypocrisy. I ran from one abusive home environment toward other adults and ranking military personnel expecting to be embraced and groomed to be a strong healthy young Man,… but what I actually received was simply more abuse because I was recognized as being extremely vulnerable regardless of the reasoning.

Based on my accounting of what despicably happened to me,… I was clearly experiencing what is presently called *Military Sexual Trauma* (MST),… which is currently defined by the Veterans Administration as:

> ***"Military Sexual Trauma (MST) is the term that the Department of Veterans Affairs uses to refer to sexual assault or repeated, threatening sexual harassment that occurred while the Veteran was in the military. It includes any sexual activity where someone is involved against his or her will – he or she may have been pressured into sexual activities (for example, with threats of negative consequences for refusing to be sexually cooperative or with implied faster promotions or better treatment in exchange for sex), may have been unable to consent to sexual activities (for example, when intoxicated), or may have been physically forced into sexual activities. Other experiences that fall into the category of MST include unwanted sexual touching or grabbing; threatening, offensive remarks about a person's body or sexual activities; and/or threatening or unwelcome sexual advances. Both women and men can experience MST during their service."(i)***

> ***"Military Sexual Trauma" is the term the Department of Veterans Affairs uses to refer to sexual assault or repeated, threatening acts of sexual harassment that occurred while a veteran was serving on active duty or active duty for training."(i)***

> ***"Experiences of MST can affect Veterans' mental and physical health even many years later and is associated with conditions such as posttraumatic stress***

> ***disorder, depression and substance abuse. MST can also lead to physical health problems such as headaches, gastrointestinal difficulties, sexual dysfunction, chronic pain, and chronic fatigue."(i)***

When I look back on my life during the past 20 years or so specifically,… I can clearly see and understand what I often felt in the heat of the moment. The internal palpable sense of shame of not wanting to be "this way",… and an almost automatically driven need to hide what was troubling me mentally. This unspoken need to hide became the motivation to not seek help in my early years of living with Mental-Illness. I also had grown up with a sense that anyone who is different in any way,… is to be arbitrarily ridiculed, pushed aside, marginalized, belittled or simply not taken seriously as a potential intelligent Human and contributor to a functioning society. Stigma in my experience does not simply emanate externally like some water balloon thrown at me,…rather,… it can and did emanate from within myself at times though unwittingly drenching my mind with a specter of fear. For me,… the internal version of stigma appears to have been more sinister and corrosive,… especially leading up to what would be my poorly executed suicide attempt and the one instance when *failure* was a life- saving "friend". All arbitrary societal programming lead me to conclude that I was worthless as a Man, Human, and undeserving of all that life had to offer. All the stigma driven self-concluded worthlessness was in the shadow of a multitude of accomplishments dating all the way back to when I first learned to walk and talk. How odd that for so many years I automatically down-played or even forgot about my endless list of accomplishments,… from the seemingly mundane to the profound…! I had to choose to help myself,…. first by seeing myself as worthy of help,… next I had to ask for help and once I did that,… so began the gradual end of the automatic application of the internal version of stigma (branding of disgrace). None of this process has been easy to say the least and Stigma is a close cousin of Shame & Guilt when it's self-inflicted. I have noticed that [**three elements**] listed below seem to be present whenever I'm engaged in unraveling issues in any major area of my life.

According to Webster's Dictionary:

Embarrass – *To make self-conscious or ashamed.*

Shame – *A remorseful consciousness of guilt.*

Guilt – *The fact of having violated law or right. A sense of having committed a wrong*

As most individuals may have already realized,… changing habitual ways of thinking, believing and behaving is difficult. In a society with a growing usage of anti-depressant medication along with a seemingly endless list of random illnesses that can lead to experiencing depression or anxiety,… it is probably a good idea for those who are not afflicted with some version of Mental-Illness at this time,… to heed the experiences of those that are currently in distress. It may be time to consider choosing the abandonment of the "sword of stigma",… so that it is not at the ready to slice through the spirit of a relative, friend, spouse, co-worker…. or even yourself at a time of confusion and distress.

Chapter 6

Accused of Being Gay

From then on, a cloud followed me throughout the military. The incident in the bathroom turned into continual and daily taunts about my masculinity and my sexuality, even though every other airman (male or female) on base was undoubtedly engaging in self-pleasure too. On that first day at breakfast when B taunted me, I should have thrown my tray down and kicked B's ass, but after years of being berated by my own father and accepting it in order to survive and avoid punishment, my first instinct when B verbally assaulted me was to keep my mouth shut. So that's what I did.—I worked hard at school and avoided fights, verbal or physical. B eventually failed most of his classes & tests and thus washed out of Tech School. Yet, my self-esteem was decimated. Humiliated and emasculated by the daily jokes and taunts by co-workers (male and female), I couldn't bring myself to write to Z. I missed her company but couldn't bear the thought of having to tell her about the harassment or having her come visit and witness the abuse by my peers. Then, one day several years later at an Air Force Base located in South Carolina, a ranking Staff Sergeant in uniform, at work, openly accused me of being gay,…in front of witnesses!

The Sergeant's insulting,'s callous and cavalier behavior was simply one more verbal reflection of many attitudes within the rank and file morally dysfunctional-collective of my Squadron / Propulsion Branch. These ordinarily intelligent senior ranking sergeants and officers had long since allowed this type of overt harassment to flourish,… without any means provided for me to right a wrong under supervision,…violently or otherwise,…so that I could maintain my dignity & career.

I intuitively knew that I could not return to my abusive *home* back in Knoxville Tennessee,… so I existed with the devastation for over five years.

In my endurance,… I lost it all,… family, career, dignity, money and sanity.

My life and existence had been made into a type of circus-side-show for the daily enjoyment of all who chose to engage in the apathetic behavior,… sadly,… there were so many who chose to be instigators & hindrance rather than help.

Keep in mind that in 1989, being gay in the United States military was a Court Marshall offence under the Uniformed Code of Military Justice (UCMJ) and punishable by Jail time, fine, demotion in rank, dishonorable discharge or vigilante-death perpetrated by other military personnel (this has happened historically on many occasions in the Armed Forces). So this was a particularly injurious accusation to make and a potential indicator of his willingness to impose vigilante-death. I firmly looked the Sergeant in the eye and said, "Do not call me gay." Yet, the Sergeant persisted. "Fag!" he said to me. It took every ounce of my patience to avoid jumping over the counter and start beating the shit out of that Sergeant. Instead, I looked up at the clock and saw that two hours of the work shift were left. When quitting time came, I walked over to the Social Action Office and brought the Sergeant up on charges of harassment. Very little was done to that ranking Tech. Sergeant (five striper) for his verbal conduct unbecoming a Non-Commissioned-Officer (NCO). Many of the same individuals (Master Sergeants) that forced him to [politically] apologize to me,… were themselves guilty of participation via jokes to some degree while I was stationed at that Air Base. For me,… my career had long since been arbitrarily destroyed before it even began…! No one took me seriously,… which is how careers are destroyed still today in politics, corporations or the military.

All it takes is a few words,… true or false,… and an individuals' career will be instantly clouded with doubt pertaining to his / her character & abilities,… with no way to prove otherwise. The proverbial Pandora-box and once it was opened in my case, it couldn't be closed,… no matter what! This is what happened to me,… a young Airman with hopes and dreams that were randomly snuffed out for a quick laugh to be had by all. The odd thing is that many of these people went on to have or already had children of their own and I imagined that they expected a better world to be waiting for their children or grandchildren. Even during one of my most daunting and utterly disheartening hours,… I was able to discern the fact that what these individuals were actually creating was a world that would potentially or eventually confront their own loved ones at a later date or maybe themselves.

The world chopped up my soul into little pieces and thus far I have made do with what was left.

I once talked about how I had been told that,… during slavery times in the American South,… my Great Grand-Mother and other individuals made do with what they were given in terms of food. When the owner of a plantation butchered an animal,… many of the parts were considered waste or unfit for consumption and often times were given to the slaves. Being creative as they always were and continued to be,… family cooks put into food,… their *heart, mind, spirit, pain, desires and ingenuity* to say the least. Once throw-away animal parts such as pig-tails, pig-ears, guts (chitlins), pig feet and ribs that had very little meat on them,… would all be paired up with other simple items such as cooked greens. In any other country these simple items would be called peasant-food,… but in this country,… it's known as Soul-Food. To me,… Soul-Food has a deeply profound meaning that goes way beyond what's on my plate. Soul-Food represents an ability to survive, creativity, genius, cleverness and a connection to Source-Energy / God under some of the most harsh conditions that one human can exact on another human. Though it has been at least fourteen years since I last cleaned a five-pound bucket of slippery foul-smelling pig guts with the business end of a butter knife,…only to end up with about two pounds of edible chitlins,… there is nothing like that nose twisting fragrant aroma of fresh pig intestine. I once shouted,…."have mercy on my nose so that my taste buds can rejoice at dinner time…!" "And don't forget the hot sauce, cole-slaw and cornbread…!" For me,…Soul-Food became a metaphor in terms of my views on relationships of all types (personal, amorous, food, health, spiritual,..etc,,.) in my life. Just like those foul-smelling pig intestines or other scraps of food,… my relationship with myself often times came with bits and pieces of "fat", "foul-smelling crap package" and a "core structure" that seemingly had no meat on it much like a slab of ribs. A Man such as me may have appeared this way while overwhelmed with dis-ease as a result of a complex anxiety disorder such as PTSD. Nevertheless,… with a little ingenuity and persistence,… that foul-smelling gut wrenching experience of dis-ease (depression, anxiety, socially outcast,…. etc.,.) had the potential to yield life-sustaining lessons that can and did propel me forward in ways unimaginable by me or others while dwelling in an often time deep darkness of despair. Take note of that individual like me that seems to have nothing going for them but bits of "meaty" character clinging to their shattered spirit,… much like a raw slab of ribs consisting of more bone than meat. Once cooked up slow and low over the fire of passion,… and forged between the anvil & consistent hammering of life experiences,… can yield a mind-blowing feast for the person who is cleaver and alert enough to see the value in themself. I found value in myself. Under the most dire circumstances,… many slaves such as my Great Grand-Mother survived,… I'm proof as such,…as I tell this story to you. I have faith that any relationship,… individualized or as a pair-bond,… can survive with a willing participant(s) and I bet on myself. Consider putting a little ***Soul-Food*** into your relationship with yourself,… and / or your significant other as I have done with myself,... one day at a time.

I have several memories dealing with Women that have always plagued and confused me. I never understood why the words and voices sting so deeply and infect my every thought of any Woman with an uneasy desire.

The first happened when at 5 or 6 years old I was chastised and whipped by my mother for being "Mannish" with my little cousin whom was not much younger,…about 4 or 5 years old. I was made to drop my pants in front of the little girl and her Mother as my Mother whipped my legs with a switch. I later as an adult Male realized that I truthfully always felt humiliated about that event and started to wonder if it had anything to do with my confusion around and toward Women. My father did the same once when I was about 7 years old because I was teasing my sister as she played with her doll-babies one day. I once again was made to drop my pants in front of a girl eventhough both I and my sister got the switching that day but she was 4 years older and laughed as I endured the punishment from my father for nothing more than trying to get the attention of my sister,… at least that was what was in my little innocent mind at the time. That was the first and last time I ever remembered my Father physically laying a hand on me in that manner and I often wondered if my Father saw something humiliating about the punishment technique that he did not like. On the other hand my Mother continued to whip me in this manner until about age 9 or 10 and as an adult I began to wonder if it was my mother's way of getting back at my abusive Father via humiliating his one and only son as a representation of her Husband. I have very real reasons to suspect such a nasty and twisted behavior because my Mother was openly jealous of my older sister Sherry because of my Father allowing her to work in the Bar-B-Q restaurant "The Place" or "The Pit" for short,... even though three other older sisters worked there also. I never understood the confusing feelings I felt when I heard my Mother express anger and jealousy towards Sherry in her presence or absence.

A third type of mal message regarding females took place when I was in first grade,… the first time. I had developed a crush on a little White girl in my class that also lived in the Walter P. Taylor housing project down the street from my house. I had spent my 25 cents to get a ring from a bubble-gum machine at Cas-Walker grocery store one day while on a shopping trip with several of my older sisters. When we returned home I asked my sisters to help me write a note to give to the little girl along with the ring but what I got startled me in a way that I would not begin to understand for many decades. The impact would create immediate and long lasting confusion towards Women of all types, colors, nationality,… etc.,.While holding my hand one of my sisters said with an anger voice,.. "why do you want to be with that White trash?!". I remember feeling confused, humiliated, ashamed and as if I had done something wrong for simply liking a girl,… at least in my mind I got some weird contradictory message that girls are not for me eventhough I wanted them; moreover this message came from Women that I looked up to and admired. Never mind the Black / White racial issues that I knew nothing of at that time as a child,… but definitely felt that I had done something wrong in a basic sense based on my sister's reaction. The next day my sisters went with me to place the envelope and note on the little girls door step. I never knew if she received it or not to this very day but I definitely knew the harsh feedback that I received once more for placing my healthy attention on females, be it my cousin of a similar age, my sister innocently teasingly or a first grade class mate that happened to be White,… the message was the same in my little mind,… "you're wrong and bad for liking girls". For the duration of my up-bringing, I never ever received any type of confirmation of my desires for girls in an age appropriate and positive manner. I did however frequently witness all the brutality that I could stand from my parent's relationship and that of my eldest sister (Jeanie) taking beatings from my drunkin Brother-in-law. Twisted sounding,… yes. Truth be told,… as an adult Male,… I have often times felt a weird and twisted sense of myself cheating / betraying my sisters and other primary Women that I grew up with,… I never understood why when I did have a date on occasion,… I felt like I did not deserve to be with the Woman or on the date period for that matter,…I felt uneasy to be with any Woman eventhough I had strong desire for and adore Women of all types to this very day. I formed such a twisted and trusting strong bond to the seven Women that I grew up around as care-givers,… that in order to be with any other Woman I feel like I'm cheating in some weird way. It's very distressing to say the least to feel faulty as a Man for appropriately and emotionally desiring closeness with any Woman other than my sisters or Mother. It's a sickening thought and feeling to say the least. As it pertains to the opposite sex,… I know that inadvertently some wires got seriously crossed years ago in that young boys mind.

In the book (Self Matters) Dr. Phillip McGraw talks about "defining moments" in a person's life and the accounts mentioned here by me are definitely a few.

I have been haunted by this country song (*Counting My Lucky Stars* by Mike Stinson) that says it all about something "wrong" feeling "right" or is it the other way around in my case when something intuitively RIGHT,… got conditioned to feel "wrong". For some reason this song kept playing over and over in my head and inspired these words & thoughts at 3am on 15 October 2012.

Source:
    (i)   VA.gov

Chapter 7

Gulf War: Trigger in a Bar Room

One day I received a "Dear John" letter from Z telling me that she had met someone else. I still cared for Z very much, but I let her go without a fight. What could I do? My silence had already done the work for me. The girl from Levi Strauss that I had fallen in love with had moved on to someone else willing and able to communicate with her. PTSD's effects had run like a poison into my love life. When the Gulf War broke out, I was sent to Germany. I had hope of an adventure,… something new,… a chance to leave all the taunting by my military peers behind me. But the very same Sergeant,… Sgt. "insult" from my squadron who harassed me just a little over a year earlier in 1989 and had called me gay was assigned to the same team of mechanics that were deployed from an Air Force base. We all flew on a cold uncomfortable C-141 cargo plane with all our equipment and supplies. We sat side-ways in web-seats with no cushions and I must have had a waffle print on my butt at the end of that long flight from the United states,… across the Atlantic ocean and finally landing in Germany at an Air base with an agent of vengeance in tow. I wondered silently to myself,… "who needs to worry about terrorist threats to charge the gate or blow-up the base when I have this man and many like him standing next to me". These individuals had convinced themselves that I was gay and they needed to do something about it and little did I know that I would soon be served up another cold hearted dish of harassment that picked up where it had left off back in the States. Of course I was in deep denial to think that anyone in the military really cared about me at that time. Many of those individuals' attitudes turned outward were just as twisted as

Hitler in terms of logic & self-loathing. The odd thing was that some were white and some were Black and of different Religious backgrounds,… but it did not matter as I painfully learned. I learned not to assume anything based on another persons' claim to a specific Religion, Spiritual path, harsh historical cultural experiences, etc.,….; I would advise anyone of this. One Master Sgt. Leading the team had a Jewish sounding name,… another was Islamic (Nation of Islam / Black Muslim). They seemed to play both halves against the middle by acting buddy-buddy or like a cohesive team that had each other's back one minute and the next minute I got the distinct feeling that I was the butt of the joke telling emanating from their mouths. Maybe I was overly sensitized or maybe not,…. nevertheless,… the humiliating jokes and laughing continued blatantly and typically off & on all day long as eyes would cut sharply towards my direction,… as if they were all searching for the slightest reaction from me. Life dished out this confusing lesson to me also.

It's a good thing that they were not carrying loaded weapons because definitely I felt that I might have become a casualty of "*friendly-fire*" / "*accidental weapon discharge*" at the hands of Sgt. "insult" in particular,…. or someone else of the same ilk. I along with others that were tasked with defending an Allied Nation (Kuwait) after the country was invaded by Iraq in fall of 1990,… was on official specific orders to be a part of a killing machine that would eventually kill, maim, and or orphan many humans that I did not know the names of,… nor had they (Iraq) did any harm directly to me,… yet I had at least one notoriously known individual (Sgt. 'insult") on my "team" and there were other men & women just like him in boisterous attitude,… if not to the level of blatant contemptuous action oriented and vivid stupidity,… like Sgt. "insult" had displayed previously. It reminded me of something I had read in a J.D. Salinger novel titled *"Catcher In The Rye"*,… were in one passage the character Holden Colfield talked about how he or his brother that was in a war with men that he was not sure of who was his enemy,… the men across the field that he was supposed to shoot dead,… or,… the men sitting next to him in the trench.

Similar to Salinger's character,… I clearly had experienced a disturbing and twisted odd sense of duty & loyalty gone horribly wrong amongst my military contemporaries. It turned out to be a rather blatant farcical level of choice made by the senior ranking decision makers to assign

Sgt. Lovely (me) and Sgt. "insult" to work as a "team" on such a critical mission and especially sense the Chief Master Sergeant of the Propulsion Branch and others were all well aware of what had happened between us two airmen barely a year earlier. This came as no surprise to me based on what the attitudes and unofficial policy to allow rude and unprofessional behavior to openly fester for many years prior to all this happening. I often retrospectively wonder if the rank & file were quietly taking bets on how long it would take for the situation to go critical as it eventually did. If this were true,… it would undoubtedly have been indication of them having reached a new status of low and disgrace for the uniform and rank insignia on all pay grade levels. The consistent disdainful professional ineptness of senior ranking military personnel that had already been demonstrated to me,… gave me reason to question their motives beyond simply that of protecting their individual retirements. They chose not to get involved early on nor put a stop to the mayhem. With me,… the serious bodily injury was taking place internally in a massive way and no one did a damn thing to stop it!

Just like when I was a child in Knoxville Tennessee!

Betrayal! I had a lot of pent up pain in me. There is just something about the idea of betrayal,…. that breach of trust on a core level that really sets me ablaze internally! My "home" Air Force base was known as an unofficial retirement base anyway,… so there was really no reason to care about anyone but themselves and many of the ranking Sergeants appeared to do just that and were rewarded with the standard retirement at the rate of 50% of full rank pay-grade. I have no respect for any of them and call into question the very essence of their Duty-Honor-Country which is part of the oath we all took when we enlisted in the armed forces. As a citizen of the United States and a member of its' armed forces,… I as well as the others had a duty to one another that obviously faltered in one direction from the very beginning. The oath I took upon enlistment was apparently an idealistic goal that did not apply to Sgt. Lovely (me) in actual implementation.

One night, in a bar, I bumped into two military peers who invited me to go elsewhere for another drink, along with one of the wives of another airman who all happened to be White. The three of them were permanent party at Hahn Air Base and I accepted, happy to have some company and appreciating the gesture of potential friendship because very few individuals Black or White wanted to socialize with me over the years. But then out of the blue one of the airmen made a crack—a masturbation joke at my expense. Instantly the hair on the back of my neck raised and that all-too-familiar eerie feeling came rushing through me. I said nothing until the group stood up to leave and then something in me snapped. I punched one of the men, seemingly out of the blue, as the woman (whom I later learned "serviced" the men on his base) looked on. When they didn't return any blows,... I knew that I had been suckered into a fight! Just like a year earlier when Sgt. "insult" had attempted to draw me into a fight at work while we both were in uniform back in the States and it didn't pan out because I was on my toes that day. But this time I was under the influence of two drinks (one beer, one bailey's) consumed during a three hour period and I soberly realized that this situation had [set-up] written all over it! Too late,... damn,... I thought to myself!

Imagine a scenario in which two immature *man-childs* taunting a neighbors' pit-bull dog get bit badly,... and then want the authorities to euthanize the so called "dangerous" dog. Maybe I was wrong that night with my assessment of the situation,... but,... maybe I was not when one considers all that I had been subjected to for many years, prior to that night. I had / have to live with the outcome either way.

A short time later In the middle of the night around 03:00 hours the military Security-Police (SP's for short on an Air Base) bammed on the door to my room in the barracks that I shared with another soft spoken, Kool, intelligent Black Man (Sgt. Calm). Calm answered the door because his bunk was closest to it and in the same instant I stated that they were looking for me. Now I walked escorted unhandcuffed,... flanked on both sides by two White males wearing badges and carrying guns. Once they arrived at the station (SP Shack),... I was asked to sign a document / statement that the other Men had written,... giving their account of the so-called one sided assault.

I sternly refused to sign any document and finally signed a affidavit that clearly stated the I was refusing to sign-off on any statements written by my accusers or comment on the incident. I was alone in the most profound sense, tired, sleepy, under duress and dis-oriented by my first arrest to say the least. By the time the First Sergeant ("Shirt" for short) arrived it was getting to be around 07:00 hours and I had been up all night; nevertheless, that morning of the next day, back at the engine shop, I was interrogated by my "superiors" about the assault. I once again found myself surrounded by no less than three Master Sergeants that were all White Males and one of them was Sgt. Zealous…!

By this time,… I smelled a for real "Fuck-Job" on the horizon coming from these guys,…. with their chests all stuck out and acting all pompous. I refused to indulge their fake supposed desire to help me and need to hear me outline the despicable story for their amusement. I detected a weird nasty glee in each of their eyes,… like funky scavengers moving in to pick clean the rotting *carcass* of my military career. So I simply stated in a calm,… yet stern commanding voice,… burdened heavily with thoughts of resignation in my heart and mind,… "Whatever you want to do to me, do it. You want to take my stripes, take them. I'm tired," I said. I said this while looking up at the standing Master Sergeants surrounding my seated position. They stood like a pack of smelly vultures,… as I rotated my head with chin up, squarely made eye contact and paused with each of them. In that moment in particular,… I knew that they,…. neither anyone else really cared about me since the very beginning(1986) based on their consistant behavior. I was no longer in denial.

There was no need to shout obscenities or raise my voice. Eventhough my childhood, career, Religious faith and trust in the goodness of humanity had all been systematically crushed like a car at a junk-yard,… something unrelated to any of these ideas and beliefs was still very active with and within me,… at another one of my darkest hours. Apparently some unknown source of strength, silently, intuitively and momentarily assured me of no need to seek aimlessly for that which had already slipped away,… simply Let-It-Go-On-Its-Way.

I had to apologize to the commanding officer of my host squadron there at an Air Base in Germany. He was a highly successful officer who was a Black Man at the rank of Major. The humiliation of that alone was a heavy blow for me!

To me it seemed relatively easier to fail in front of a White Man,… who arbitrarily expected nothing more than failure from me,… but astronomically painful & difficult to fail in front of another Black Man,… who arbitrarily expected nothing less than success as a mandate. Either path was littered with mental anguish, pressure and a journey of enormous levels of humiliation to say the least. But given a choice,… I would always chose the risk of the later as I had worn my uniform with a sense of Duty-Honor-Country, pride and a can-do-attitude while under duress of personally epic proportions. I acknowledge that it was humanly impossible not to have found myself in error from time to time. Maybe these feelings and beliefs were a direct result of my childhood training and thus I before him and so on right back to slavery. I have come to believe that my attitude is potentially part of what makes a Bratha such a formidable figure in society or a beacon of despair much like myself. The enormous pressure can mentally crush the body but the *Bratha* will always be standing if he chooses from the inside,… and this too,… has been demonstrated historically.

Throughout history Brathas have reached into thin air as a resource and created their minds vision from the seemingly impossible and often times humiliating circumstances of all types.

For me,… standing in front of that commanding officer,… was if I was starring my father in the face,… the father that for years had told me in so many words,… you're worthless.

I got an Article-15 punishment under the Uniformed Code of Military Justic (UCMJ) that consisted of confinement to the base for thirty (30) days. Basically it was a type of house-arrest in which I could not exit the gates of the base for any reason, and had to forfeit fifty dollars of pay ($50) per month for three months. Although I was well aware of the fact that I had dodged a serious bullet in terms of punishment,… it was of little consequence considering that my heart, mind and sense of masculinity had already collapsed. No commander could have dished out any pain worse than that…

The PTSD had taken its toll on me. All the teasing I had faced and my body's relentless descent into a state of distress and psycho-physical chaos had worn me to a thin thread about to break. I was generally barely functioning in life and at work, but now I was coming undone from the inside-out,… I knew and felt it in my gut. I also knew that there was absolutely [no one] to turn to for help. Once again, I had an eerie sense that I was *Living-a-strange-death.*

Living A Strange Death

From my death I breathe,
From my death comes agony.
From my death I walk,
From my death I talk.
From my death I am Bratha,
From my death I know no other,.... way.
From my death I live,
From my death I give.
From my death I know no other,…. way.
From my death I speak these words true,
From my death bear witness,… all of you.

By
Howard Lovely, Jr.
29 November 2012
7:31pm

Chapter 8

Unraveling

Six months later, the day I returned to the United States with fellow airmen at Columbia Regional airport in South Carolina and within five minutes of leaving the airport to return to an Air Force Base, I got pulled over by a racist police officer. Sgt. Got-It-Together had brought my car to me and we were both shocked at the fact that the officer stood by while I dug through my duffle bag to retrieve my state-side driver license. The police officer did not care that I had just returned from Germany in support of the Gulf-War. The message was blatant, yet unspoken and profound: "Fuck You!... Sgt. Lovely",… for all your patriotism and team-work. I still have that traffic ticket in my old foot-locker with other military paperwork. The incident further disturbed me as I was already feeling distraught over the hypocrisy I witnessed every day as the men on my team,… the men I was supposed to be fighting with and be able to trust,…made fun of me. Once back in the States, an experienced Black Sergeant named Got-It-Togther took me "under his wing". "Have you gone over and apologized to the Commander?" Sergeant G asked me, in reference to my having punched the airman while overseas. I looked at him and said, "No, I didn't think I had to." Sergeant G looked back at me sternly and said, "I strongly suggest you make an appointment to see the Commander and offer an apology." And so, I did. But it was devastating for me. A few days later, I walked into the Commander's office, with my pressed camouflage battle-dress-uniform (BDU) uniform on, did a left-face turn, stood at attention, and saluted my female Commander. "Sergeant Lovely is reporting as ordered, ma'am. Ma'am I'd like to apologize for my behavior in Germany. You sent me in to do a job and I made a mess." It was one of the hardest things I've ever had to do. My Commander was not only a woman,… but a Black woman,…a Major in the U.S. Air Force from whom I wanted to earn respect. "Apology accepted. Dismissed, Sergeant," said the Commander, releasing me mercifully, as tears welled in my eyes. I saluted, did another left-face turn, and forced myself to escape in an upright posture before my tears rolled out, but I felt torn to shreds. Feelings of failure swarmed all around me like annoying nats,… just like they had for all those years when my father would tell me at report card time,… "You've got to do better".

Once again I felt torn down from the inside out in front of a Woman,… as I so often felt as my Father had consistently criticized me in front of my mother and sisters. As I left the commanders office with my stomach in a knot,… my face was as tight as a drum,… and my body was chilled as if there was not an ounce of spirit or blood left in me. I maintained my oscar winning performance as I silently convinced myself that I was fine and walked across the breeze-way back to the Propulsion Branch where I worked. At times during that day my mind was like the frothy surf at an ocean beach and just as disgusting smelling. I was getting tired mentally and my sense of masculinity was plummeted to depths beyond which I had ever experienced before and I had been very emotionally low prior to this event. My sense of reason was fading fast and out of control as more and more,… my body betrayed me,… system by system.. I didn't know what to do,… or who to turn to for help with my ever growing tsunami of turmoil washing inside me. It was a relentless wave after wave that left my external life in slow motion shambles. All my Religious beliefs,… respect for rank and file,… respect for myself and desire to continue on in this life time started to melt in a contorted mess much like a cheap candle that easily disintegrates from the heat of the flame. Everything around me including myself began to appear extremely cheapened and worthless.

The strips and stars on my and other airmen's shirt sleeves,… officer bars, oak leafs, eagles and stars began to take on an appearance of something less than their intended honorable representation. The ranks of Mother, Father, Older Sibling, Uncle, Aunt, Family Unit & Church had long since graced my heart and mind with falsehoods about loyalty, honor and support,… while simultaneously and blatantly abandoning my need for help. I'm tired and ready to leave this place,… I thought to myself,… I've seen enough.

I found sleep, food digestion, mental concentration and the will to persevere to be increasingly difficult in the face of some unknown internal foe that continued to drain the very essence of my existence. I had begun to feel an internal isolation so vast that the entire milky-way star system could fit inside my heart,… and not be detected.

Chapter 9

Suicide Attempt

One night after work, I packed a gym bag with some clothes, threw it into my car, and started driving. I was tired, tired of all the crap, tired of people who were supposed to be on my team,… yet belittling me, tired of feeling alone and scared, tired of the sore muscles and stress that came with being on guard all the time, tired of showing up each day with my pressed uniform, my shined boots, and a smile on my face and I was damn tired of feeling like there was no way out. So I drove without knowing where I was going. I drove for two days and nights straight through South Carolina, North Carolina, and Tennessee,… stopping only to get gas and sleep in my blue 1985 Mazda RX-7 sports car. Then I stopped in West Memphis, Arkansas, and checked into a motel. I had driven right past my sister's house; neither had I stopped at my parents in Knoxville. *I'm all alone,* I kept thinking. *Nobody is going to help me,* I echoed as I booked a room at the check-in desk. Then, sitting on the edge of my bed, I thought, *I just want to end it all. I want the pain to go away.* So I walked over to the closet, secured my belt around the rod, stuck my head in, and pulled on the belt to test things out. It was uncomfortable, and I wasn't sure if the belt would even be enough to kill myself,… so I went back to the side of the bed to think. Then I remembered that I had Sergeant Got-It-Together's phone number in my wallet. I could call him. When I did, Sergeant G knew it was me right away. He told me everyone was looking for me. To me his statement made little sense considering that by all indications,… no one gave a damn about me in the first place. He asked if I was thinking of killing myself? He got me to commit to driving back, knowing that I was

a man of my word and would follow through on my promises. "Man,…
I'll tell everyone you're coming back. And,… Howard, you keep in mind
that not everybody dies when they get in a car wreck, sometimes they
get mangled up,… paralyzed." "You drive back through those Smoky
Mountains, safe." When I heard that word "paralyzed" over the phone,…
I couldn't help but think how socially, career, dating,…etc., *paralyzed,*….
I had already felt during the previous five years,… how mentally mangled
I had felt during the nineteen years leading up to my mental melt-down.
Sgt. G was talking about the physical,… but I was already vastly steeped in
a mental *wreck* in which a fireman's jaws-of-life tool couldn't pry me loose.
I had been in a type of mangled up psychological *wreck* for a long time by
now. In addition to that,… some individuals at my military base were just
now starting to take notice of my distress and act "*helpfully*" toward what
had been blatantly in their face for many years. Technical Sgt. G had only
been stationed at my Air Force base for about two years and was attempting
to clean up,… or more like do damage-control,… for a mess that had
been left unattended by his contemporary Master Sergeants and officers.
Sergeant Got-It-Together was a very physically strong featured Black Man,
with blackened skin like coal,… similar to the look of my Grand-Daddy
who was the son a African slave in Tennessee.

TSgt. G was very intelligent, organized, confident and experienced in
life. If only he had offered to help me sooner before all this had happened,…
if only I had met him at another military base,… maybe,… just maybe he
would have groomed me unlike many others that chose to tear me down,…
both Black & White,… young & old,… male & female. Everybody seemed
to rush in to "*help*" at the time when they could do the least to help me and
understanding my dilemma. This fact didn't inspire me towards trusting
any of them much at all. Somehow deep inside myself I knew that they
all were just protecting themselves at that point. The rank & file had to
act fast because now they had an airman under their direct command,…
unaccounted for and not present for duty,… AWOL in military terms,…
Absent-Without-Leave. That situation had to be explained up the chain of
command,… one way or the other. You'll not see this serious offence in
my military records because the commander had chosen to acknowledge
the situation as more of a medical emergency rather than a disciplinary
offence. Under article-15 of the Uniformed Code of Military Justice

(UCMJ), a commander has wide latitude of punishment options. Because my squadron commander (Black Female) Major SG had chosen and acted with intelligence, good judgment and compassion, I was allowed to dodge a dishonorable discharge, reduction in rank and prison time to say the least for the AWOL offence alone. However at that time in my troubled "life",… I could not even contemplate the legal enormity of my actions based on the fact that was not thinking clearly due to my extremely intense mental duress.

I felt like powerful winds of a violent thunder storm or hurricane,… had ripped through the *branches* of my mind and toppled my strong masculine physique. Much like a 4 foot diameter solid old oak tree violently ripped from the earth intact,… and tossed to the side. In a mental state of duress such as that,… I could feel the roots of my weakened mind vulnerably exposed to the human elements of contempt.

My up-ended *mental-roots* dried up so rapidly that not one tier was available to quench the profound thirsty need for help,… yesterday,…last week,…last year or at any time prior to and including the present! How can anyone replant a *mind-tree* of that size & age I ask!!!? How, when and where will I ever replant myself?!

Many years later I would figure out that what I actually wanted when I was suicidal was to release the mental torment that I had been experiencing. I did not understand its' origin or why it held me hostage with such relentless zeal. I actually did not want to die. I wanted freedom from within my mind.

There was something about the long drive from West-Memphis Arkansas to my Air Force Base that gave me time for reflection. The sound of the car engine was soothing to my senses in a strange way and the alone time with no other voices or offensively obtrusive energy offered a retreat of sort that would be short lived once I returned to the base.

Chapter 10

Sent Away

I checked out of the motel just a few hours after I had checked in. Then I drove my exhausted body and aching mind all the way back to the Air Force base, in and out of two more days and nights. I showed up at Sergeant G house, where the Sergeant had told me to go straightaway. "You got no friends at the barracks," he had said. I didn't feel like anybody cared for me at this point anyway and I felt conflicted like I always did while growing up with my parents who were both my care-givers and tormentors. I was once again simply taking what I got as I did with my parents. "You come stay with me." said Sergeant Got-It-Together. Him and his wife took me in and I slept on their couch for a week, while the Sergeant and the chain of command mercifully worked to handle my situation as a medical one rather than one requiring disciplinary action for going AWOL, which could have easily led to a dishonorable discharge. Sergeant G paraded me through the Component Repair Shop (CRS) Propulsion Branch hangar where I worked to let everyone see that I was back at the base and to also do what needed to be done to avoid me getting an Article 15. Everyone seemed to be working to help me now, but maybe that was just the politically correct thing to do. The support felt like they were all a damn day late and a dollar short. Why hadn't anyone stepped in before now? Why hadn't anyone taken me under their wing and mentored me prior to that moment or punished the men for taunting me? Just before I stepped onto a Cargo plane set to take me to another Air Force Base where I would be admitted to a psych-ward on the base hospital's 4th floor,… Sergeant G told me,… "Go on and live your life, man.". I guessed that the rank and file figured that they all had successfully gotten rid of their problem and TSgt. Got-It-Together would have delivered the report as such.

Chapter 11

Admitted

The exact date is lost on me, but I do remember that I put on my Dress-Blues and boarded the white painted hospital plane that landed at Shaw Air Force base just to pick up me.

How's that for limousine service and "royal" treatment.

I do remember that it was a warm fall day in August. I remember that because I was wearing my short-sleeve dress-blue shirt. It was the middle of the afternoon when the plane touched down at an Air Force base and I felt a mix of hopefulness, apprehension, disorientation and shame to be there. I was alone and unescorted once more in my life at a time of distress and when I most needed guidance. I had to summon all the remaining sanity that I could call upon to fill out paperwork at the intake station at the airport as my duffle bag was brought in and checked for proper identification. Within a few minutes of me arriving,… a tall young twenty-something Black Man showed up in a white short-sleeve shirt, white pants and black shoes. He resembled an image straight out of a Holly-Wood movie,… only I was not Jack Nickleson (One Flew Over The Kookoo Nest) or Robin Williams (Patch Adams).

Naw,… this was Sgt. Howard Lovely, Jr. (Star of his on Real-Life-Breakdown-Drama aka SCREWED).

The psychiatry ward at air base hospital was all shiny and reflective: waxed floors, white walls, tile everywhere. And damn, it was cold. They had that air conditioning turned up so high it could freeze a polar bear. On the 4th floor ward the nurses' station was surrounded by glass and the other patients stared intently at what was undoubtedly a handsome, intelligent, accomplished Black Man looking sharply dressed externally but obviously internally riddled with shards of unseen glass. The result of a shattered heart, mind and soul that led me to wonder,... *what kind of "weakened" & demoralized man of any physical stature manages to stand tall with his knees planted firmly in the floor and the soles of his feet facing upward,... a Man with his mind all blown,... a man with his heart all crushed,... a Man with abundant unchecked confusion roaming through his soul,... enough distress to share with ten-thousand other people,... where does my strength come from I thought to myself? When I thought that I could never take another step toward any endeavor,... I took a half step. Something inside me would not let me [choose] to quit! By the time I appeared on that hospital ward in fall of 1991 at that Air Force base,... it had been 19 years since I watched my Father threaten / attempt to kill my Mother and vice versa on numerous occasions.*

Down in the deep recesses of myself,... wherever the mind resides,... my mind knew that by age eight I had literally dodged a bullet by no more than 24 inches,... a bullet that was intended for my Mother. By age nineteen I had literally side-stepped a butcher-knife blade by less than 6 inches that was intended for my Dad...!

I had endured a potentially neck snapping head-lock as a nonviolent interference act of defiance toward my Father by stepping in between the fighting adults in order to shield my Mother. In the time frame of five seconds if it were five minutes,... I dodged a knife blade from my Mother & a potential neck snapping from my Father. The odd thing is,... I did nothing wrong as a 19 year old young man. As a matter of fact, I did everything that my parents asked of me,... to a fault,... and was met with disapproval most of the time particularly from my Father. I was obedient / loyal to both parents and it damn near got me killed by [three] individuals! Although I did nothing to instigate the ruckus between my parents, I would eventually realize that I paid a heavy price for their foolish behavior. At the time of the writing of my story that you are reading, neither parent nor anyone from the Family has offered an apology for their thoughtless and reckless actions that put me in peril at the hands of my own two parents. Additionally,... my Father is deceased so that rules out any potential apology from him.

With all my experience and consistent haunting memories,... I had no clue that those childhood days that I had spent under near constant & daily duress,... were at the center of my present day circumstances while checked into a psych-ward at an Air Force base in fall of 1991. Unfortunately unbeknownst to me at that time,… it would be more than two additional decades and thousands of hours of tolerated inadequate psycho-therapy,… mostly via the Veterans Administration before I would be properly diagnosed and treated for PTSD by a civilian therapist. I would also endure countless day & night time hours of anguish and side-effects such as involuntary muscle movement (tardive-dyskinesia) from at least one medication; this simply added another layer of humiliation and embarrassment by providing visible physical movement to my hidden mental turmoil.

As I walked the floors or hung-out in the rec room with other patients, board out of my mind and I spit out just enough words to the therapist in group sessions to earn myself a pass to go outside,… that familiar feeling of humiliation dogged me constantly. Only it was deeper now. I was a Buck-Sergeant in the U.S. Air Force,…a three-striper with a star for Christ's sake and I had let everyone down. I had lost my marbles and been taken off the job. But I wanted help so I shuffled through the psychiatric stay, even as that humiliation followed me in and out of my bedroom, down all those corridors, into the shower, around the dining hall, and out in the courtyard during other people's smoke breaks. So why couldn't the doctors and nurses and therapists help me? Why did they (nurses & aids) take only fifteen or thirty minutes a week to talk to me one-on-one? The remainder of the entire two months stay consisted of the staff attempting to force me to talk about my feelings and issues in a group setting that felt very un-safe and not personal at all for me. The weekly group meetings consisted of Men and Women with some dealing with Bulimia, anorexia, drug use, steroid use, and paranoia associated with work place ethnic difference in the case of one captain that was of Middle-Eastern ethnicity. I myself was struggling with emasculation, paranoia, work place harassment / Military-Sexual-Trauma (MST). The professional staff literally expected me to open up about my feelings in a [forced] group situation. When I look back on it now with the ability to put words to the situation,… I can see that it was drastically inappropriate, inadequate and unrealistic to expect a Man such as me to openly talk about what I had been put through at the hands of other military rank & file. It was ridiculous to say the least. Why didn't they help me when I told them that the medication,… the stellazine, wasn't working? "You have to give it time to work," they said. I realize now that I was sent to that Military Psych-ward at that Air Force base as a precursor to the eventual ending of my military career and the rank & file knew it as such when they sent me there under the idea that it was supposed help. They were just getting rid of what they viewed as a problem and threat to their careers considering that they had done nothing to stop the crap (MST) from the very beginning before it lead to my mental break-down. I began to see this as especially potentially true for the individuals that were nearing twenty (20) years or more toward retirement. If this would have gotten out back then,... the idea that the rank & file actually knew and were aware of the duress and harassment that I was being subjected to daily,…they themselves would have been in serious trouble for potential derelection of duty,..punishable under the Uniform Code of Military Justice (UCMJ). Could it be that I wasn't having paranoid delusions, as they had diagnosed, but that something else was going on? If that was the case and something in me told me that it was,… these doctors never took the time to find out. Two months after my admission to the military psych-ward in 1991, I was released and honorably discharged from the military. I felt as terrible as ever, and the diagnosis on my out-processing paperwork said, paranoid delusions-*persecutory type*.

What,…. if anything was paranoia / delusional about what I had been through as a civilian or Sergeant…?

Chapter 12

Chasing a Dream: Going Back to School

"Dad, can I come home for six months?",… I asked my dad from a pay-phone on base. For the first time in my life, my dad didn't yell or criticize,… he just said "yes." Still, I was ashamed. My dad had always berated me for joining the military,… if I would have told him that I had ended up in a psych-hospital and been discharged (even though honorably), what would he have said? I kept it all inside, walled off from my father and all the family's eyes: my going AWOL, nearly hanging myself with a belt, the two-month hospital stay, the delusional diagnosis. The scenario was a replay of my childhood days where I was in pain and no one seemed to noticed,… only this time I was choosing to hide what I actually was aware of about myself. The fear and hiding of PTSD continued. Six months passed and then I was gone from my parent's home in Knoxville, trying to find my own way again. In 1992, I borrowed my brother-inlaw's truck and drove down to Daytona Beach, Florida. I started classes at the prestigious Embry Riddle Aeronautical University. But after one semester, I had to drop out due to lack of money, so I went back to Knoxville and enrolled at the University of Tennessee. But that didn't work either. The continual episodes of full-fledged PTSD impaired my focus and made it almost impossible to concentrate; two necessary elements for completing courses were severely disrupted at that time. Then there was the summer as a counselor for a children's camp and one more attempt at school as I drove west and enrolled at a Community College thinking that the extreme environment change would "fix" me for the umpteenth time. Would I ever complete my dream of getting a college education?

When I arrived in Seattle Washington in February 1995,... it was about two feet of snow on the ground if it was an inch. I was disoriented, tired and in full PTSD mode; I was rittled with anxiety to say the least. I'm not able to remember the exact date I arrived in Seattle but it was a few days before my 31st birthday and I did not know anyone. For my birthday I took myself out to a strip-club (RazzMatazz) that was not too far away from where I was staying in a rooming-house. I had been long since starved for the wonderful Female attention that I adored so much; so I made it a point to casually let one of the Ladies know that it was my birthday. While she was giving me a lap-dance she engaged me in conversation and asked,... "what brings you here tonight?",... I've never seen you here before."... I answered,... "well I just moved here and don't know anyone and it's my birthday today". That was the political answer I gave the lady,... but just beneath the surface I was really scared, lonely, confused about my life thus far and desperately needed answers to my mental ailment more than I needed an attractive intelligent half naked Woman. This is not to imply that I didn't appreciate the opportunity. Well the very next song,... I found myself being lead on stage by every Lady in the house and was encouraged to sit in a chair, on stage,... while all the other Men looked on with envy. All the scantily clad wonderful smelling Women danced around and rubbed against me in such a way that I wished it would never end,... the tension in my body had disappeared. The anxiety from the PTSD had vanished! My mind was momentarily refocused and the pleasure center of my brain was triggered. The exact same central nervous system that was causing my anguish 99% of the time,... was now excited but with different thoughts, fantasy and anticipation. Moreover, I got a different result even though it was only temporary. Although I would begin to notice this pattern in my body, I was seemingly powerless to change it permanently. I found myself imprisoned within my own body.

It was one of those "ut-o...!" moments that lead to more questions than any answer. If I was trapped in my own physical body,... then were is Howard?,... Who is Howard?,... What shape or form is Howard if I am not my physical body,... yet merely stuck in it?

Different Kind of Prison

The kind where I am the warden.
I am the trustee.
I am the inmate.
I am the guard-ian.
But most importantly I have realized,
I am the *governor* of my *state* of *mind*.
I have been in prison long enough.
I choose to pardon myself!
I take control of my fate.

By
Howard Lovely, Jr.
July 3, 1998
5:35am

"Are you fucking kidding me!?",… I thought to myself. "Focus on all these Ladies and their beautiful plump or flat asses,… look at her G-string Man!" "Look at her Breast Man!" "Look at her smile!",… "no!",… "The other *smile*!"

This sort of "split" thinking and awareness happened often in terms of my physical body going one way and my mind in another direction with complete sensory awareness of both at the most inappropriate times. As if there is a best time for this type of confusion. Maybe it felt like I had two separate brains simply because my two halves (right & left hemisphere) were not communicating properly,… as I would later learn?! In any case,… that night and many others similarly,… My brain was awash with a temporary self-imposed "therapy" that triggered the pleasure center of my brain in such a way that part of me had forgotten all about fear! My eyes saw beautiful Female eyes, my nose smelled the sweet scent of perfume and natural female hormones,… my ears heard the whispers of a multitude of soft Feminine voices honoring me as a Man and my skin was delighted by the brief touches of the Feminine form!

The music suddenly stopped! Damn, the fantasy was over! I returned to my Table located front and center of the stage where I stayed for at least an additional hour more after paying a $15 cover-charge and repeatedly paid,… $5 for a coke,… $20 for a lap-dance,… $40 for a private lap-dance and $20 for a shower-dance. That night I must have spent $500 dollars for about two hours of psychological relief in the form of Female attention; my own personal brand of "therapy" eventhough it was rooted in fantasy and extremely short lived.

That $500 dollars was the monetary equivalent of real therapy sessions at the approximate rate of $140.00 x 3.5 hours / sessions,… minus the music, thrills and $5 coke!

It was a boost to my ego even if it was just a night of fantasy!

The experience also solidified my feelings of existing in a physically out of control body that was not functioning congruently with my mind and central nervous system.

Reality quickly set in as I left the strip-club late that night with no job prospects,… no Female companionship,… not yet enrolled in school and no real direction in terms of how to permanently alleviate my near constant psychological pain.

I later enrolled in the University Of Washington but that lasted exactly one semester due to my inability to concentrate just like I had experienced at the University Of Tennessee and Embry-Rittle University before that.

I seemed to be running in circles alone while desperately trying to get answers from the VA Hospital there in Seattle but all they gave me was a bottle of pills (Haldol) that did not aid me nor lessen my mental pain. The pills did give me tardive-dyskinesia (involuntary muscle movement) that fortunately went away after I took myself off the medication without the doctor's permission. I recognized the symptoms from literature that I had read; the clinic gave me the literature along with the pills. I was not willing to let myself get fucked once more,… by waiting one more month,… to allow others to make the judgment call of weaning me off the medication. By that time I could have potentially had permanent muscle spasms I surmised,… and an additional problem to manage alone.

I finally enrolled in an aviation maintenance program at a community college where I struggled alone to stay focused each day and pass each *test,*

both academically authorized and the socially sick and un-ethical forms of tests.

I eventually graduated surprisingly with a 3.62 grade point average, Honors graduate, entered the National Deans-List for two years (1996 – 1998) in a row and was inducted into Phi-Theta-Kappa National Honor Society of two year colleges.

All this was accomplished under extreme mental duress and with an empty feeling on graduation day. I wrote the following poems in my journal just a few hours before attending graduation ceremonies in excruciating mental and physical pain that felt like shards of glass beneath my skin:

"Glory"

This glorious moment,
I can't feel the fullest.
Achieved not by my father or he before him.
But given the support,
The love and encouragement,
I will stand as a beacon,
A dream or hope for those who follow,
This night,…of all nights thus far,
College graduation night.

By
Howard Lovely, Jr.
19 June 1998
3:02pm

"Body"

Aint afraid of nobody,
But my body's pain.
Words of others',
But my bodys' pain.
Actions of others'.
Denial toward me.
But my body's pain is what I must conquer.

By
Howard Lovely, Jr.
11 June 1998
4:05pm

Chapter 13

Losing Dad

It was certain now; my father would never see me graduate from college. In January of 1994, my father went into cardiac arrest in a hospital parking lot after being discharged because the doctors didn't deem anything wrong with him. Bottom line is,… those ole White doctors didn't give a damn about my 64 year old Black Father,… end of story! Here is how the story began. I received a call from my youngest sister, letting me know that Dad was coming home to Knoxville for the weekend for a visit. That was it,…no mention that Dad had called them and asked to be picked up from Chattanooga or that he had told them he wasn't feeling well. So there I sat all weekend long in my apartment studying for classes at the University of Tennessee, just a few short miles from my childhood home and the dwindling hours of my father's life. But I didn't know my father was sick; I only knew that chances were strong that if I went back home, I'd hear Mom and Dad fighting. Some years back, Dad had moved to Chattanooga where he had an apartment for his weekday job as a USDA meat inspector, and he and mom had been mostly estranged since then. I just couldn't take the vicious cycle or arguing,… not anymore, not now that I was a grown man and could make my own choices. If I had known my daddy was going to die, I would have done something differently. The call came in the late afternoon on a Sunday, again from one of my sisters. I rushed over to the hospital and I and the family sat in the waiting room until midnight. The pronounced alkaline aroma of the hospital smelled of death I thought to myself and the specter of PTSD was dutifully by my side as I fought to hide it. The bright fluorescent overhead lights hurt my eyes as always and the mirror like waxed floors were a constant assault to my senses from below. This Man that had constantly proclaimed that I could not do anything without his help,… lay helpless with tubes and electrical wires attached to his body in a desperate attempt to prevent the inevitable. That six foot two, proud and intelligently capable Man called Father,… had been reduced to that which he always proclaimed to me and he couldn't even help himself at that point. When the doctor pronounced my father as dead, I hit the hallway floor bawling,… back against the wall while inhaling massive amounts of the tell-tale hospital smell of death. One thought whispered through my mind: *"I'll never hear it now. I'll never hear dad say he's proud of me."*

For the third year and January in a row since my suicide attempt in 1991,… life had shown me death in a very personal way. This included the very young in my 19 year old nephew in January 1992,… of whom I Baby-sat as a Teen one summer, my 38 year old sister in January 1993 of whom I was fond of and now my 64 year old Father in January 1994 of whom I admired. This too has always silently haunted me to this very day. It has been like a twisted Charles Dickens tale with a title that might sound something like this: "In the Wake of *Your* Death"

Chapter 14

An Accomplishment, in Spite of

"You're going to be on medicine the rest of your life," the psychiatric nurse told me. She had given up on me,… like all the other professionals. But I hadn't given up on myself. "No, I'm not," I quickly retorted in a respectful but firm tone. I didn't know how I was going to get better, I just knew I would. And that's when I told myself, *"Either you're going to figure out a way to kill yourself and do it right,… or,… you are going to take one step forward every day".* I chose the latter. On June 19, 1998, Howard Lovely, Jr. walked across the graduation stage with honors and induction to Phi-Theta-Kappa International Honor Society. Somehow, in spite of the anxiety attacks that ripped through my body on a daily and often hourly basis, I had earned my two-year degree, with honors. Next, I undertook the grueling, two part oral & practical A & P (Airframe & Powerplant) licensing examination. I passed again in spite of a body and mind that were constantly malfunctioning. As a result of earning this license, I was authorized by the FAA to perform mechanic tasks independently, sign off on my work and sign off on the work of other non-licensed individuals' that I had observed the work of. I got a job performing heavy-maintenance(D-Checks) on primarily 737's and MD-80's via an third-party maintenance facility and bought myself my first house. A house! It was only 10 years old and I would have 1,025 square feet of my own. But I wanted a companion to share it all with and I couldn't just up and buy myself a wife. So I went to the dog-pound after finding Gracie's profile on the internet.

It was a Monday, and I had taken off from work. When I got there, Gracie ran up to me, all jumping and sloppy wet kisses, and I decided she would be the one I would share it all with, at least for the foreseeable future. *"I can't take her now"*, I told the handler, *"But I'll come back Friday."* All these years later,… I still have Gracie,… now 14 years old having survived death-row, a rattle snake bite, a car roll-over, two surgeries to remove tumors and now has arthritis. Gracie takes doses of Gabapentin & Tramadol that I have to shove down her throat daily. Gracie has been a great Life-Saver-Companion and tolerated my ailment when the rest of the world would not. I may have "rescued" Gracie from dog-pound-death-row,… but she has saved my life on many profound levels. "It was the best $25.00 that I have ever spent",… that was the adoption fee at that time. Now we are both old and grey haired in the face.

Although I generally enjoyed my work on the aircraft rather than the dysfunctional corporate environment, I was only able to maintain employment at the Aviation repair facility for about 3.5 years; the entire time I continued to get worse mentally and physically with breathing problems that eventually landed me on medical leave of absence in the spring of 2002. I eventually resigned my career and explored additional civilian help to resolve my mental health issues. I realized that something core in my life was drastically wrong with my thinking in terms of working sick to pay for "things" such as a house, nice new truck, money, prestige as an FAA certified mechanic, etc.,… rather than having my health be at the center of my life with all the other stuff mentioned above as secondary aspects that support me in a healthier way. I made a drastic decision to let it all go by selling the house. I called a local church to come and get most of the furniture and then I set out to do internal work in California which lasted 5 years. I noticed that sometimes the heated pressure of illness and life can have disastrous effects on an individuals' career & healthy life progression in general.

In nature we can see recently with much of the United States having been in a heat wave for 60 - 90 days this summer of 2012. This warmth in small metered amounts is great for plants animals and humans; however, in massive continuous doses,… the same environmental stress can cause damage of all sorts such as stunted plant growth, medical emergencies with humans and drought. For example,… in my own garden I have yellow crook-neck squash planted along with a few other heat tolerant summertime favorites such as eggplant and pole beans. My kentucky-wonder pole beans only climbed half way up the fence, many died and none have produced beans at this time which is peak season in my garden,… this week my eggplant (Black Beauty) finally put out one "fruit" the size of a silver dollar so far and my yellow squash plant is producing 1 to 3 "fruits" per week when normally I would be over-run with 1 to 3 squash every other day. This is a simple example how stifling stress can be.

Now,… let's imagine that what I have out-lined above is a metaphor for an anxiety disorder such as PTSD:

Human Brain = plant / muscle
Heat = anxiety / stress / event
Stifled Growth = disrupted social life, employment, family, health…etc.,..

In my life,… stress resulting in PTSD or a Complex Anxiety disorder has acted like a massive long-term "heat wave" adversely affecting my internal [brain environment]. It has stifled my ability and mobility in my social life, dating and employment. With plants and humans,… stress in small amounts can actually be a good experience in terms of encouraged adaptation and or growth that is typically beneficial; however, extreme amounts of stress whether acute or chronic in duration can cause the opposite effect. Weight lifting is a common example. If I lift a small amount (10 pounds) of weight doing arm curls and gradually increase the weight (15, 20, 25, 30, 35 to 40 pounds) over an extended time period,... my muscles will adapt and grow stronger even though microscopically the muscle fiber is being damaged and repaired automatically by the body's own powerful self-preservation system. Add too much weight too fast and the result can be catastrophic with a badly torn muscle that will cause limited or no use of that muscle until it heals. Sometimes plants never recover from stress. Likewise my brain structure (neurotransmitters) continues to adapt to stressful situations from the time I was born; however,.... much like the plants subjected to an excessive amount of heat due to a heat wave,... or my muscle subjected to large amounts of weight too rapidly,... my brain also,... somehow can be "torn" or "stifled" in terms of proper neurotransmitter communication ability. My "torn" brain has been invisible for the most part, disruptive in every area of my life imaginable and physically & emotionally painful to say the least.

Chapter 15

Never Going Back to the VA

Once I was labeled paranoid-schizophrenic by the VA doctors and psychologists, the diagnosis stuck. As a result,… for many years,… the VA medical community had me pumped up on antipsychotic drugs that didn't work. Instead of getting better, my symptoms worsened. The sound of a coworker running a rivet gun at work, the bark of a neighborhood dog, a friendly honk of someone up ahead when the light turned green all triggered me into fight-or-flight mode hundreds of times each day. And every time I asked the VA doctors and therapists to reconsider my schizophrenic diagnosis, they wouldn't budge. I knew something was wrong with me, but the label the doctors had given me didn't seem to fit. It certainly wasn't helping me heal. One day, shortly after a two-week self-admitted stint in the VA hospital psych ward because I was wanting to end my life again, at 31yearsold I sat in the office of the VA psychiatry department head for an outpatient visit. They had switched psychiatrists on me yet again, which they seemed to do every six months with only a week's notice, just when I was finally feeling comfortable with the new therapist that apparently were all just passing through at my expense. "You don't trust me, do you?" the grey-haired White doctor asked me. "No," I replied tersely. "I think you're smarter than people give you credit for being," the doctor continued as he scribbled something on his pad. Did he think I was faking? Or did he detect that I knew more about myself than he or the doctors gave me credit for. "The pills aren't working," I said. "Well, we've got you on the highest dose," the doctor responded confidently. *"But the pills aren't working",* I thought to myself, as I took the doctor's scribbled prescription and my anger flamed. "See you next time," the doctor said as I walked out the door. "This is bullshit," I thought to myself. And as I stood in line to fill my prescription of government-supplied pills that didn't work on me, one thought kept running through my mind: *"I aint ever going back to a VA doctor / therapist"*.

Webster's Dictionary gives one definition of *frustrate*: "prevent from fulfilling plans, hopes, etc.,".

During the first 33 years of living with what I now know was / is Post-Traumatic-Stress-Disorder,… from age 8 until 41,… I had a lot of frustration. I felt like I was falling short in everything that I attempted to do from attending grade-school, college and everything in between that you can imagine. I felt so unheard, misunderstood, judged, labeled and lost in most areas of my life to say the least. Most of this time I had no idea of how to explain my feelings or challenges to friends, work colleagues, family, etc.,.

What did I do to overcome such frustrations???

The best that I can tell you is that I simply grew through it. The feeling of frustration has never gone away for me to this very day,… but I amazingly have achieved many major goals, regardless of the constant frustration that I have experienced while living with a mental illness. When I stop and really take an honest assessment of my life at age 49,…. it does not look exactly like I had planned,…. not even close, but I do have a few things to show for my forty-nine years. Let me put this another way,… imagine that you and me are acorns sprouting beneath the ground. Now think of the [resistance of the dirt] as being "frustration" to the seedling as it inches its' way through *darkness*,… toward *day-light*. Then it finally breaks through the surface and it still has a lot of growing to do. This is the way my life has been prior to and starting seven years ago when I had a breakthrough with EMDR. The EMDR allowed me to breakthrough a type of *darkness* that I had lived with for many decades and I'm still growing. So the next time I or you feel frustrated,… think of the seedling that eventually grows into a 400 year old oak tree due to [persistence] if nothing else. Take note of what you have achieved even if it was a little bit of self-care yesterday in the form of showering, eating and or getting the mail out of the box, etc.,… that's what I did at times,… that's all I could do for myself on many occasions. Although the frustration may never go away, make like an acorn seedling and keep reaching for the breakthrough. Keep persistence as your constant companion and grow from the inside-out,... that's what I did to move through frustration.

Chapter 16

You're Not Crazy, You Have PTSD

How...to...survive...trauma. These four simple words graced the cover of the book that one of my civilian therapists in Seattle leant to me from shelves of books in his office back in 1997. Later, I moved to a cottage by myself in the mountains of California. I had resigned my job in Washington State at a Aerospace company because I had spent many of the past years waking up in the middle of the night, unable to breathe. I suspected my respiration problems came from all the chemicals, although my employer hadn't been willing to take responsibility or to help me. But here was a book that maybe could. Each of the words on the cover was short,...no longer than two syllables,...and yet they held so much weight. In fact, they changed the course of my life. As I turned the book's pages, one by one, the puzzle pieces of my shattered world started to fit back together. A syndrome was described that I had never heard of before, PTSD (posttraumatic stress disorder). Suddenly, everything made sense: the sweaty sheets after a night of fighting through sleep, the continual adrenaline bursts throughout the day every time I heard a loud noise or someone or something came too close to me, my feeling of isolation from the people around me. I was *not* schizophrenic; I was like the soldiers and survivors of assault and abuse described in the book in front of me that had posttraumatic stress disorder. A very normal and real response to the horror and helplessness that I had experienced as a child when I watched my father nearly kill me and my mother. Now that I knew what was potentially going on in my mind and my body,... was there hope that I could recover from the disorder?

Much of what I read sounded as if I could have written it myself based on my experiences and feelings. I often felt that my body and mind was being torn apart or at least going in two or three directions simultaneously,… for example there is this thing that I call "freeze-ups". Freeze-ups would happen while driving, working, talking to a prospective date or anywhere. My physical body would continue to do whatever activity such as driving but be very tense muscularly, yet still mobile,… my mind would be split into two behaviors that I was well aware of. There would be the part of my mind that was aware of my environment and body posture and there was the aspect of my mind that was stuck / frozen. As I approached a stop light or stop sign,… the "frozen" mind would see the green light turn yellow but my foot would not move from the gas to the brake. As if this was not enough,… my other part of my mind that was aware of my body movements desperately and silently struggle to make my legs move from the gas to the brake petal,… this internal battle seemed to feed on itself at times. Somehow I was able to get my right foot on the gas and on to the brake while still engaged in a "Freeze-up". I would bring the car to a stop,… the light would turn green but my eyes and mind were still fixated as if staring off into space. Of course the driver behind me would sound the horn and my skin would tingle from the sudden shock, my heart would race faster but I would continue driving. Sometimes the shock of the horn would snap me out of the "freeze-up" and embarrassment would set in as my heart pounded my chest. This type situation happened routinely at work, school, driving, on a date, on the phone, or in public at the checkout counter while grocery shopping and sometimes someone would mistake my stare as if I was looking at them but I was not. But they didn't know that.

I often was accused of day-dreaming in grade school when the same scenario would happen a lot. It's a wonder that I even graduated high school let alone college…! The grade school teacher would yell at me with the resulting similar effect much like the sudden sound of a car horn mentioned earlier. I could not repeat what I had visually seen on the chalk board or heard my teacher say just seconds prior,… even though I saw and heard every word spoken while in a "freeze-up" state of mind. Of course embarrassment set in often in grade school when this repeatedly happened; shame also definitely cut deep into my self-esteem as a young boy. Now,… I am a grown Man that has the experience and words to tell this story of how my body & mind betrayed me repeatedly since age eight. Recounting all this stuff about "Freeze-ups" reminds me that a few months ago I was asked the question:

"What does being "conscious" mean to you Howard?"

After thinking silently for a while,… I came up with the following answer for myself.

When an individual is aware of his / her behavior and establishes congruency between thoughts, words & actions by making small internal adjustments consistently,… this is consciousness. Driving a car, flying an airplane or riding a bicycle are good metaphors for this "Spiritual" / "Religious" process because keeping either one "lined-up",… requires the operator to make small consistent adjustments based on changing road / environmental conditions,… that can throw the vehicle off course.

Keeping this in mind,… I think of my body as being the metaphorical vehicle.

Then I took the metaphor to a whole another level and asked of myself:

Where is the "Me" / "Operator" in the equation of Consciousness??

Where is the first person pronoun "I"…?

Who is the "I"…?

What does the "I" look or feel like…?

As if this wasn't enough of a "noodle" baking question,… I then turned around and asked myself:

"How does any or all of my Spiritual / Religious concepts and beliefs encourage or hinder my recovery process…?"

"Do I fully understand in the smallest of ways,… the seemingly complicated Laws that govern my profound existence in this physical body at this time?"

It is said that Jesus said,… "As a Man thinks,… so shall he become".

This concept is expressed in many other sacred text and oral traditions,… though with different words.

If I were to interpret this Law literally,… it will infer that I somehow asked for PTSD or so did another individual stricken with Cancer, MS or any type ailment,… somehow asked for it. I do not believe that the Spiritual Law works that literally. Yet I do have personal evidence in my life that the Law does work generally. It's kind of like attempting to understand the concept of [air] as a life-giving force / gas without seeing it physically,…

yet knowing it works generally to keep my body alive,… and without air,… I would have certainly died. Electricity is another conceptual example that exists with profound impact within and externally of my body,… yet it's existence and location is difficult to explain or pinpoint. It's simply everywhere all the time and profoundly powerful,… just like the power of Spirituality / Religion of all brands. Each person can choose to Plug-in to the [resource] or not. I chose to reconnect.

I do not really understand what this all means in terms of my "freeze-ups",… but something is definitely odd to say the least.

I still wonder,… who the hell's in the driver seat…?!

I often times refer to being caught in the *middle*,… or "freeze-ups",… as living a strange "death". I often feel,… that I am observing my body and experiencing sensations via my body,… while simultaneously not in control of my body,… or even in it for that matter. I think that this alone,…is enough to drive any person bonkers to say the least.

Recounting these specific situations,… reminds me of many aspects of my journey thus far,… including having read Edgar Allen Poe's exploration of this idea of being stuck between life & death in his tale of *Mr. Valdemar*. I wonder if Poe somehow had a form of anxiety himself and attempted to give it voice via many of his tales that contain themes of being trapped in a torturous internal battle. Considering that modern psycho-therapy has only been around since the 1950's,… surely one of the only and best therapists Poe would have had at his disposal,… would have been in fermented liquid form,… and the proverbial couch would have only been needed once the booze took effect.

As I started attempting to understand what I now know is,… and has been,… undiagnosed PTSD up until August of 2005,… I have discovered many painful facts about my feelings and life. One thing that seems to go back really far is the idea and experience of [abandonment]. As a child,… when the guns, knives and angry words would so often surface between my parents,… I had no vocabulary to describe what I was feeling as I watched and listened in horror,… as early as eight years old and up until age 21. At that time my skin tingled daily and furiously for 13 years during my childhood from 1972 – 1985 and beyond,… a feeling like a thousand mosquitos had descended upon me all at once to suck the "life" out of me and my groin pulsed as if I were about to wet my pants most times,… but

I never did. Maybe it would have been a relief mentally if I had wet my pants,… or simply an indicator to the adults that I was in urgent physical & mental distress. On these occasions My mouth became like cotton,… my ears as sharp as a bat detecting the action & sound of a gun-bolt long before my eyes gazed upon the flash,… my breath intermittent and muted,… my eyes as keen as a hawk that has zoned in on its prey (my parents) and yet my feet and some part of my mind were rapidly frozen without my willful choice,… like an opossum or mouse trying to avoid the clutches of instant death. In all this foolishness at best,… I discovered abandonment on many profound levels.

I would later realize that stigma & shame came with this package of daily horror and is really society's way of "abandoning" anyone for any reason.

My parents abandoned good judgment, me, themselves and worst of all,… My mind abandoned my physical body and got stuck behind the *curtain (PTSD)*,… or more of a feeling of existing somewhere *in between*. The "in between" feeling is what I call "Living-A-Strange-Death",… an eerie state of being both [present] and simultaneously [absent] with full unrelenting awareness of both. I call these moments [*freeze-ups*],…and they got me in trouble with my grade school teachers all the time for so-called "Day Dreaming",… it hurt to be accused of not paying attention over and over again and I didn't understand why my young body continued to dissociate (clinical term for *freeze-ups*). As a child & adult,…. these *freeze-ups* randomly happen all the time while doing just about anything such as taking a test, driving a car or installing rivets on an aircraft which scared the mess out of me while behind the wheel or holding a rivet gun at full blast; nevertheless, I was able to maintain composure somehow. For me,… PTSD is often times so silently horrifying that I often wondered what the hell might have happened to Edgar Allen Poe,… the master of fictional horror tales minus the blood & gore. Edgar Allen Poe explored this theme of being stuck between two worlds (a world of the living & a world of the dead) in the tale of "*Mr. Valdemar, (1845)*". The idea / condition of being stuck between two vivid states of mind sounds weird and impossible, yet I have painfully lived it for 40 years and still do not fully understand the phenomenon. Ironically my own experience of existing in my body that will not / would not function properly no matter what thoughts I commanded,… drove me *mad* and to the brink of suicide years ago. I did not want to die,… rather I wanted the physical pain & mental torment to stop and suicide [seemed] like a viable option at that time.

Similarly,… being stuck in a lifeless rotting corps tormented Mr. Valdemar in Poe's tale.

Behind the PTSD (Anxiety Disorder) *curtain* you will often find interesting, intelligent, compassionate, creative, spiritual / religious, non-religious, accomplished, socially upstanding, socially competent, kind-hearted, Uncles, Dads, Moms, Brothers, Sisters, Sons, Daughters, Aunts, Husbands, Wives, Significant Others, Neighbors, a few Ass-Holes and Capable Individuals much like I think of myself.

What's behind the *curtain in your life?*,… choose to take a look,… you may be pleasantly surprised about what and who you discover. I found a wonderful,… yet internally tortured and intelligent Man,…within myself.

"Glass In My Soul"

With every step I take,
I hear a crunching sound,
It is the glass of yesterdays' break,
What will I do?
I haven't any shoes for my mind,
Open wounds and all,
I stand tall,
And I do press onward,
The weight of my load centered upon me.

By
Howard Lovely, Jr.
April 1, 1998
3:30am

For me,... there was a high price to be paid for the externally bloodless domestic violence that I grew up with,...a violence that ripped through me internally and "bled" out my soul. I sum it up with the following painful realization in words that state in and of themselves,... I will have to carry to my grave,... the torturous revelations that the words bear.

"Price Tag"

I can't return the breath I last took,
I can't return the mental babble of the crooks,
I can't return the childhood stolen,
I can't return the pain so swollen,
I can't return the future that never was.
I can't return the landscape of my mind,
I can't return such horrible crimes,
I can't return from where I've grown,
I can't return *Home*.
I can't return my madness,
I can't return *Home*.
I can't return my sadness,
I can't return *Home*.

By
Howard Lovely, Jr.
19 Sept. 2011
5:53pm

Chapter 17

Late Stages of PTSD: When the Body Turns on Itself

I now knew what disorder I had, but life was still difficult, very challenging. Although I had moved into the mountains just south of San Francisco about 30 miles, a type of isolated country setting and left my job near Seattle back in Washington in 2002, my internal chaos would not resolve. PTSD's appetite was insatiable… it would find me wherever I was. One day, in the garden, I was digging through soil in my containers, when a hummingbird flew past me and hovered over some nearby nasturtium flowers. Buzz, *buzz, buzz, buzz.* Buzz, *buzz, buzz, buzz.* Those hummingbird's wings flap something like twenty times a second. And they were loud, damn loud like a giant bee. To my body that was always ready to pounce, always ready to implode like a demolition of an old building, those wings might as well have been as loud as the launch of a fighter jet into the wild blue yonder. My body flew into full fight-or-flight mode: heart racing, hair standing up on the back of my neck, muscles tensing to brace against some invisible intangible haunting horror that was ever present in my mind and skin. My body had an agenda of its own, independent of my intellectual desire for some sense of calm or normalcy within myself. My body instantaneously felt like how a crumpled aluminum can looks,… smooth in some places, but contorted, stiff and easily torn apart with sharp cutting edges left behind in other areas. Nature mimics this behavior in terms of geologic processes as tectonic plates shift around causing earth quakes, tsunamis and even land deformation with both subtle and dramatic results such as the formation of mountains in some cases. The inside landscape of me had been in an up-heeval for over three decades by this time,… with devastating and life altering results. On this occasion,… I calmed down,… eventually,… but a short while later, while sitting in my armchair, my stomach gurgled. I was hungry and my stomach made a noise for God's sake. That's all,…a little noise! But my mind and body were so worn down, so decimated from years of PTSD without any relief, that these common body sounds threw me flying down the adrenaline rollercoaster once more in the same day,… within hours of the first event previously mentioned.

My future looked grim; unless I could escape my own body, I could not escape the PTSD and gain the coveted,… yet elusive internal peace,… while dwelling in this corrupted body.

I felt trapped with no fore seeable way out…!

I wondered if my cardio vascular system had been damaged by all the cortisol and adrenaline that constantly surged within me daily during many decades since childhood.

I wondered when the heart-attack would hit from all the stress.

I began to question the need for a retirement account when I did not expect to live to see my fortieth birthday. "What's the point of it all" I said to himself with a calm non-suicidal,… yet resigned voice? I never really knew what true surrender meant until that point,… I had embraced and yielded to my painful predicament with intellect, realism, practicality and a great sense of aloneness just as the day I was born. Unknowingly,… at that very moment,… I had reconnected to a great core concept via this tumultuous process. The only peace that I ever gained,… was when I respectfully let go of all that I had been desperately clinging to,… including my life. It's an irony that I had to die one way or another in order to reconnect with "Life-Source". Maybe that's been the whole point to this despicable and emasculating journey.

All of my life had become difficult and unbearably painful. Even a common trip to grocery shop had long since became a futile exercise in psycho-physical pain management and simply an endurance endeavor to continue feeding a body that would not function properly. What the fuck is the point to this sick cycle I often wondered…?! That's when I started having grocery items delivered via a local service called PlanetOrganic.com. That service was instrumental in helping reduce stress levels associated with everything that was involved with shopping. From the driving in traffic, to the actual multitude of external stimulation such as smells, sounds or anything imaginable. It was as if everything and anything from dating, to shopping for clothes, to socializing and beyond was a moot point because enjoyment was not a possibility under the dire circumstances. It just didn't make sense to continue trying to force the pain to go away! So I surrendered,… and in my moment of surrender,… a door opened. Since the retirement money in my Fidelity account was no longer needed for *retirement*, I was free to use it as a last ditch effort to crack the code of the mystery that had plagued me horribly for so many years since age 8.

I define Freedom: (Find-Redeeming-Effort-Evolving-During-Optimum-Moments).

I had discovered another irony,… that the best and most favorable moment to be potentially set free from my *tormentor* was found at a point when I chose to set myself free by surrendering all,… in a mental state of resignation. Thus my mind and money were free to be used as instruments towards my eventual beginning to recover after more than 30 years of mental captivity.

All (money, help, ideas, and relief, potential,… etc.,…) became *instantly* available to me when I stopped mentally clinging to all that I had,… including the torment. I had discovered the role of the *self-observer* that many spiritual gurus speak of & that many individuals pay hundreds of dollars to learn in weekend workshops yet still don't get the point,… I observed this last bit so many times on occasion in weekend workshops that I threw myself into,… in search of answers. Life's hammer and anvil painfully forged one key skill that I needed,… awareness. Ironically it arrived via PTSD.

All conscious human change is based on this one core skill that had been blasted into my mind since childhood via Trauma / PTSD and is a tremendous irony that the intense awareness created by such Trauma has become a key factor in my eventual recovery. I had begun to consciously choose to alter personal behavior / thinking patterns to improve my life,… clinicians called this Cognitive Behavioral Therapy (CBT). I had paid a heavy non-monetary *price* to learn these lessons. I paid with my near constant apprehensiveness, dread, suspicious and frightened feelings. I paid with my social withdrawal, alienation and detached sense of belonging anywhere in the world including the childhood home in which I grew up. As an adult I paid with my near constant feelings of vulnerability, tenseness, edgy and excessive sensitivity to external stimuli. I paid a heavy price with my constant feelings of mental & physical agony, exhaustion and flat out,… outrage toward my family, parents, Spiritual / Religious community and the world in general.

I needed to find a way to provide for myself several critical non-tangible items: acceptance, appreciation, compassion, self-respect and safety from my torturous mind.

I needed to cultivate a sense of autonomy and meaning from all that I had endured thus far,… internally & externally.

I needed to mourn the realistic and difficult to comprehend loss of my entire family in the manner that it took place. I sometimes asked myself,… "What is *Family* anyway?". I realized that the definition of family is one that I would have to re-define for myself. No longer would it be a default definition primarily based on biological relations.

I needed to learn to celebrate my newly minted clarity via the self-expressional vehicle of my voice. A voice that I always knew I had because it was the one element that consistently got pointed out by being oppressed and repressed. Like two neon signs,… oppression & repression directed my mental traffic over a cliff,… against intuitional better judgment and visual reference that the *yellow-brick-road*,… was to the *right* side,… not the left.

My body compass had a missing needle rather than a bent needle!

Navigating the world by the seat of my pants was a daunting task to say the least but somehow I have managed. My body had turned on itself in a terribly painful & complicated process, spiritually disintegrated and contortedly morphed back into the distinct conscious essence of a person that I faintly remembered prior to eight years old. That was about as close to re-incarnation as I could ever imagine myself experiencing. The proverbial *do-over*,… but with the wisdom of a 49 year old Man.

Talk about being *born again*…! Having the psychological awareness of being simultaneously the one *giving birth & the born*…!

What a mind trip!,… and no drugs were involved!

There were times when I furiously pounded my fist on my old sturdy oak teachers' desk,… I paid twenty-five dollars for it at a yard sale. It's a desk that is solidly & perfectly built for this kind of agonizing writing.

At other times I screamed at the walls in my down stairs office as tears streamed from my face,… and I watched the paint *crinkle & peel*. I wasn't sure if it was the stench of my breath or the stench of my thoughts, words and anger,… nevertheless the walls seemed to *melt* from the emotional *heat*. At times like that I was always grateful to be alone in my expression of pain;… the walls could be *repainted*,…unlike my childhood.

Chapter 18

Treatment: Gambling on EMDR

I was sure that I would die in the next few years. "I'm finished," I thought, expecting a heart attack to be my end. How could my body possibly survive the hourly assaults of adrenaline that the PTSD continually launched against it? Then, I remembered a couple of books that sat out in boxes in my garage,… they were described a treatment called EMDR(eye movement desensitization & reprocessing). Was there some answer in there for me? Could anything save me from the pit of hell I had found myself living in? A friend of mine knew of a therapist who worked with PTSD patients and conducted EMDR. I chose to call the therapist. "How much do you charge?" I asked. It was a hundred forty dollars per session. "I've got forty-five hundred bucks in my 401K," I told the therapist. "How many sessions will that get me?" We did the math and it turned out to be: something like thirty sessions. That might be enough,… enough treatments to save my life. So I gambled it all, the last dollars and pennies of my savings, to see if I could live again.

With this decision to gamble on myself,… I often considered both the absence and the simultaneous possession of control in my life to be a baffling and profound paradox much like a green leaf on a tree flapping in the wind. The tree has control of the leaf in so much as the internal biological process of photosynthesis but simultaneously has no control of the movement of the leaf due to a gentle breeze which is an outside force. It's spring time and that means new growth visually and a type of "letting go to grow", in the plant and animal world. Last fall the trees turned various colors from bright yellow, orange & red to earthy brown, then crisped up and fell to the ground. The grass and most other plants did a similar shedding of the old in preparation for new growth months later. But before we all can see the visual effects of spring-time growth, the inner activity of a seemingly "doing-nothing" tree or plant,… and in this case,… me,… has been subtly busy from the inside out. A lot happens internally all winter during the so called "dormant" period. What if I began to think of my life, mental illness and time alone in isolation at home, as a type of weird human dormant period. I thought this on many occasions. A seemingly vulnerable nakedness of sorts,… much like the silent and leafless tree branches in the middle of winter standing alone as an individual,… but still among many other silent trees. I'm capable of sprouting new "*leaves*" within my mind,…. and I will socialize and converse with other individuals at the appropriate time much like the chattery whispers of tree leaves in summer time. This is how much of my personal healing process has been thus far,…. that is to say,…… shed a little bit,…. renew and grow a little bit,…. etc.,. It's a seemingly long process with profound rewards of inner beauty,… and an outer spectacle of a colorful "*leaf-life*". There is an old saying that that I was reminded of as I continued to heal my life mentally and otherwise: "A bird weaves its nest by going and coming". Because I had bird feeders in my backyard and the occasional robins' nest,… I knew this *saying* to be true in the most practical way possible based on [observation], yet I could only speculate about its deeply profound implications in terms of my human predicament and the role the concept has played in my healing process thus far.

I haves began to believe that being healed is not a "destination",… but rather,… much like the process necessary for the completion of the bird's nest. It's not something for me to achieve and then saturate myself in for the rest of my days.

Healing is potentially an enormously gentle and slow process that alternates subtly between *healed-days* & *challenging-days, healed-moments & challenging moments*. I have to discern which days are which for myself and break out of the "*shell*".

Chapter 19

Starting Over

As the EMDR treatments unfolded over a period of six months, my brain began to rejuvenate and rewire itself. One by one, the severity of my symptoms of PTSD started to diminish. In the morning when I woke, my sheets would be dry, indicating I had slept without the kind of nightmares that pushed me into a sweaty fit. A hummingbird would land in the garden and my body didn't surge with adrenaline on occasion. A car would backfire and my heart didn't launch into racing mode every time. My left brain apparently began to moderate the input from my right brain. The EMDR treatments were helping me to forge new neural connections. My body began to mellow.

For the first time since I was eight years old, I got to experience what it felt like to walk through life without the sense that some man-eating beast was waiting for me around every corner. I was forty-one years old, complete with at least half of my life, maybe more, but I had been given a second chance. A second chance at life! What would I do with this next phase of living? What could I handle? Could I work again? Could I date? Could I find true peace and happiness? Could I help other people with PTSD find the help they needed? I didn't have all the answers, but I knew one thing for sure,… I would keep on persevering to do right by myself and others. I would keep on using my intuition and my intelligence to guide myself, and this time my body and mind would support me rather than betray me.

So,… several years later I began to take a realistic assessment of my financial predicament,… "after all,… at 49,… I'm one year away from being able to register for Association of Retired People (ARP)". I started with my earnings data sheet that I receive each year from the Social Security Administration. Considering that I actually started working between the ages of 6 & 7 in the family restaurant back in 1969 / 1970,…. at nearly 50 years old I have one hell of a work-ethic and 500 shares of an aviation stock worth approximately fifty dollars in my Fidelity retirement account. That account was depleted in 2005 at age 41 to help pay for EMDR therapy as I mentioned earlier. I used all the cash for Eye-Movement-Desensitization-Reprocessing (EMDR) treatments that appear to be still having a positive affect by helping to reduce longstanding symptoms of Post-Traumatic-Stress-Disorder (PTSD). I currently have no health insurance other than that afforded an Honorably Discharged Veteran and my altered eating habits which I consider my own basic brand of "health insurance". However I tend to steer clear of the Veterans Clinics for basic check-ups or dental care,… so in essence,…. it's just available in a major type emergency if I ever need it. I maintain monthly financial obligations by utilizing the monetary compensation that I receive from the Veterans Administration to the best of my ability at this time.

What it feels like to start over after 40 years of living-a-strange-death with what I now knows was / is Post Traumatic Stress Disorder,… is a bit like waking up from a nights' sleep and feeling confused as to whether I'm still asleep or awake. It also feels weird in the sense that often times I felt like two people in one body most of the time. I am not talking about a split personality,…. it's a clear awareness of the before and after. Let me see if I can explain a little clearer. Imagine myself as a swimmer in the water just blubbing along,… I know I'm in the water and I can feel the water against my skin. Now simultaneously imagine that I'm the water also. In this scenario the water represents my past and the swimmer represents my s present. I clearly am aware of both at the same time. I'm still swimming in my past simply because it's all I know primarily, It's all my brain is programed to know intimately, until my new beliefs and behaviors take root solidly. Then I will know both the old and the new feelings. It's an eerie situation to say the least. I can tell when I have improved / lessened symptoms such as tingly skin. This chilled skin feeling happened all the time during the past 40 years but I also have a clear conscious understanding that my body has no legitimate reason to be in "fight or flight" mode based on current environmental stimulus. In situations like this that happen often, I'm both observer and the observed and it's an unsettling feeling to say the least. My sympathetic nervous system simply goes on auto pilot and all I can do mostly is observe the feelings within myself. Sometimes in moments like this, I find myself looking at my naked out-stretched arms as I rotate my hands to palm up, palm down, and back again several times in search of those tingly bumps that arise on my skin. I'm amazed when there are none lately. This silent and alone celebration has happened a thousand times if it has happened once during the past seven years of my recovery process. Sometimes I even feel joyous tears well-up in my eyes, as I look around to ensure no neighbor is watching, if I happen to be outside. On a few occasions when this happened and I was inside letting my joyous tears freely flow,… the door-bell would rang,…shit!!! I would quickly splash cold water on my face and dry it in an attempt to hide the obvious, before opening the door. Who wants to see a 49 year old man answer the door with tears…?! Especially if it's one of my snot-nosed neighborhood kids wanting their bicycle tire aired-up…! That will go over real well. Those kids are so observant and this actually happened once and the little seven year old asked if I had a cold. I played it off as best I could by saying no and then distracted him with questions about his bike problems. My emotions calmed down as I helped the little boy repair his inner tube.

I guessed that's why children and images of cherubs are similar,… they have a natural way of shifting a Man's feelings in a very un-expected and comfortable way.

That's all the more reason to protect the little brats.

I have the proverbial "do-over" opportunity with one major caveat, I get to do everything from this point forward with the wisdom of five decades under my belt in terms of this culture & world.

Having said this,…. let's add on top of this scenario the aspect of attempting to socialize with children or adults.

The act of focusing on another individual's words in conversation while constantly aware of my sensory type dual existence compounded my task and was be frustrating. If my frustration showed through via body language then I could and often got a negative feedback loop of worry within myself. As frustrating as all this must sound, and was, the joy came from knowing that my symptoms are different now and continue to get less severe since my EMDR treatments in 2005. I continue to have weird night-terrors that typically involve me alone in my old house where I grew up,… but not always. The dream scenario has always been such that,… I'm unable to get away from this unseen presence that I can feel all around myself and doors close on their own when I attempt to leave; moreover, I get chills in the dream every time this happens. The chills in the dream feel very similar to, if not the same as what I now know is a "fight-or-flight" response. I have come to realize that this type of repeating dream represents the push-pull that I felt as a kid when my parents would fight. The doors closing specifically represent my internal self-governing obedience that prevented me from running when the fighting started with my parents and the chills represent the very real fear that I felt as a kid. Now,… if I put the two elements together, I get a very intense feeling of being stuck or frozen physically which is exactly what happened in real life experience as a child, as well as in my dreams. My tears even got stuck as an 8 year old boy and never flowed until I was about 35 years old in a therapy session. When these horrible memories come up now, I cry often and get very angry as a grown man even when I feel ashamed to do so. Usually I feel good afterward for some odd reason that I do not fully understand.

Part of being a Man is under-standing myself and the functioning of this physical form that I'm in, this will allow me to understand others also. I had to modify my ideas of masculinity because of many of my experiences and the subsequent belief changes have elevated the definition of masculinity for me personally. Part of masculinity is comprised of mental strength. Finding and welding the courage to embrace the general and sometimes involuntary functioning of my body's systems such as the sympathetic nervous system, when juxtaposed to my learned beliefs about masculinity, becomes a profound journey into the realm of unmitigated courage, strength and ideas of masculinity. This must be measured from within each individual.

I learned that my cultural definitions or beliefs around masculinity has nothing to do with how my nervous system is designed to function; however, my definition of masculinity has a huge impact on how I chose to address issues of emotional processing for my overall health, well-being and optimal functioning in society.

Part of starting over at mid-life is about learning to take good care of myself by cultivating a balanced eating life-style that for me, consists of approximately 70% fresh fruit and vegetables, 5% fowl, 5% red meat, 5% dairy, 5% grains, 5% legumes and 5% selective junk-food. I gradually worked up to the way I currently eat over a number of years beginning many years prior to my EMDR treatments. In the beginning it was a way to attempt to moderate my mood via blood glucose control considering that I'm diagnosed reactive hypo-glycemic. My body simply seems to function much better in many ways and I can pretty much eat whatever I want in moderation. I sleep better, have better mental clarity and bowel movements are regular and with ease. Apparent Allergies to peanuts, grape fruit, bananas, etc., have all but gone away. It seems as though my body functions completely different without the internal mental & physical stress. It's as if I am a new person all together after gradually being revived from living-a-strange-death for 83% of my life. I'm learning to get used to feeling in a way that I have never felt for my entire adult life thus far and a good 62% of my childhood.

I'm beginning to feel alive.

People invite me to socialize but I often decline due to an inner feeling of mistrust.

The apprehension is partly a mistrust of myself (body) and partly a general lack of confidence in the humanity around me based on what I've been through during the previous decades.

The absence of a supportive family adds a great sadness to my recovery process. I can't go back to the same family dynamic that still exists in many ways to this very day. I had to make this conscious choice two years ago after finally being honest with myself about the fact that my family refused to support me all these years, for whatever their individual reasons, even after I gave them new information about my diagnosis. Starting over alone this way at 49 is oddly similar to being born in 1964. Either way it was / is an alone journey at first and maybe I will find or create a new family.

I'll keep my eyes peeled.....

The long term financial impact of what I have been through breaks down like this in a quantified manner:

During the most recent ten-year period from 2002 until 2012, I have been unemployed 99% of the time.

From 1991 through 2001 I was unemployed 55% of the decade.

From 1982 through 1990 I was unemployed 6% of the time.

The [over-all unemployment rate] from age 18 to 49 (present) is 60%.

Currently out of thirty (30) of my adult working years,… I have struggled to maintain [**consistent**] **employment** 40% of the time.

According to "standards",… by my late 40's to early 50's,… I should be hitting my stride career-wise and on target with retirement savings. Not so in my case due to my personal struggles with various aspects of Mental-Illness that includes: depression, anxiety, PTSD and elements of agora-phobia. This is a basic snap-shot of the devastating financial impact that Mental-Illness has had and continues to have on my personal life. Now all the general public / you have to do is basically extrapolate this data or pattern in terms of my life and the lives of millions of other individuals living with various forms of Mental-illness. You may begin to see an extremely disturbing National problem / trend concerning the financial impact that Domestic Violence & Mental-Illness potentially has on this country as a whole. Having said all this,… keep in mind that I am an educated (formal & informal), intelligent and highly skilled individual that has been stifled by stigma, consistent lack of support in general & Family, ignorance on my part and ignorance on the part of the medical community to some degree for 40 years,… regardless of my educational background. In my opinion,… this pattern has got to change for myself and others if the country wants to thrive. I am doing my level best with the resources that I have at this time and that includes writing this Book. Rather than remaining silent on what is a very devastating issue for me and other individuals, families and the country as a whole; I have chosen to tell my story in hope that it will at the very least instigate a serious national dialog and dispel stigma & myths.

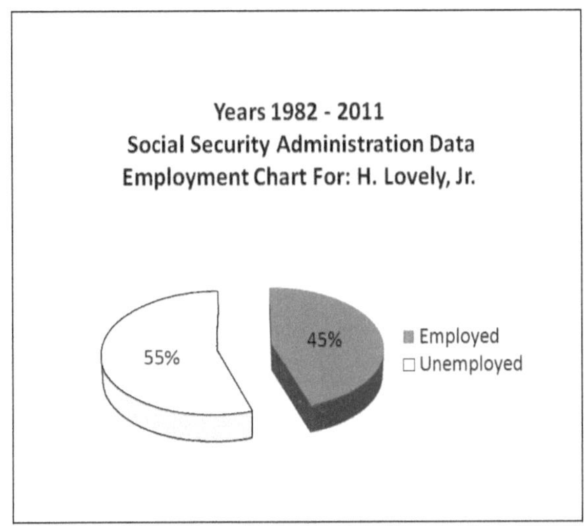

Years 1982 - 2011
Social Security Administration Employment Data

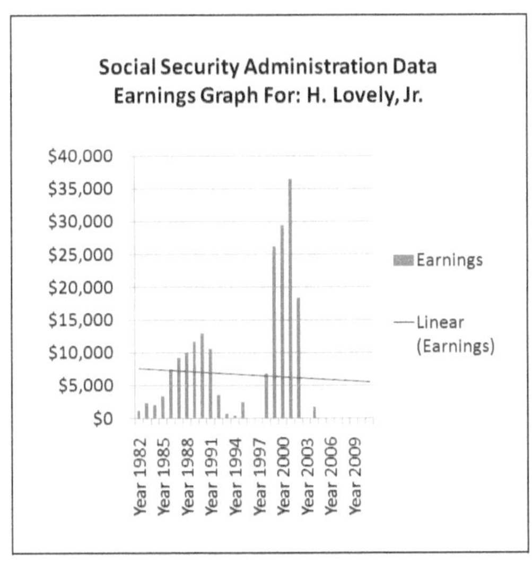

Social Security administration Data
Earnings Graph

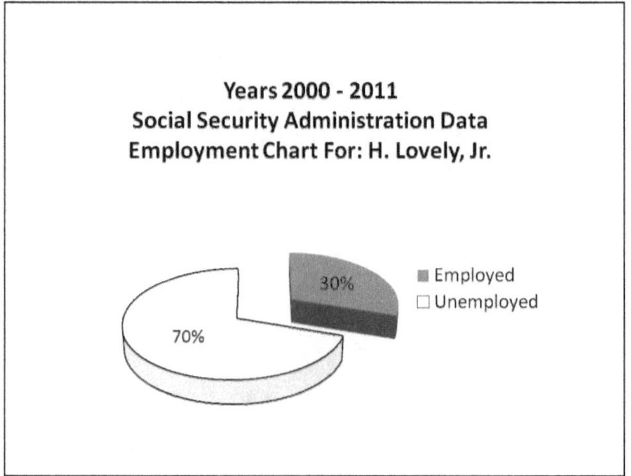

2000 – 2011
Social Security Administration
Employment Data

A Narrative of What Was Happening In My Life Coinciding With Earnings Graph

1972 – 1985 - I was raised in a very violent home environment. Graduated High School, attended Walters' State Community College in Morristown Tennessee and enlisted in USAF.

1991- Suicide attempt & Discharge from military, subsequently my personal income dropped approximately 95% in the 26 month period between 1991 & 1993.

1992 – 1995 - I attended Embry Riddle Aeronautical University in Florida, University of Tennessee in Knoxville and University of Washington in Seattle.

1994 - Hospitalized at Veteran Hospital in Murfreesboro Tennessee due to suicidal episode.

1995 - Hospitalized at Seattle Veterans Hospital due to suicidal episode.

1996 – 1998 - I attended South Seattle Community College where I earned A.A.S. Aeronautical Technology, A&P License, Maintenance Certificate, maintained a consistent 3.5 GPA, Deans' List both years and honor graduate. All this was accomplished while under psychological Distress (anxiety, depression & respiratory difficulty).

1998 - Acquired employment with GoodRich Aerospace ATS in Everett Washington north of Seattle.

1999 - My earnings ($26,231) exceeded my highest Military pay (year 1990) of $12,945 by more than twice as I continued to painfully function under emotional duress (anxiety) each day.

2002 - I continued to feel worse emotionally and physically and took Family-Medical-Leave for 13 weeks and subsequently formally resigned under duress and failing health (respiratory distress, depression, anxiety, isolation) and sold my house in Mount Vernon Washington north of

Seattle. Those necessary choices disrupted my housing situation which is critical to any kind of recovery process.

2004 - acquired employment with LockHeed-Martin in Sunnyvale California and worked for approximately two weeks before surrendering to anxiety & depression.

2004 - I used all of my 401K retirement savings to attempt healing / relief with EMDR therapy.

2004 - I filed for bankruptcy.

2006 - I moved to Colorado for an opportunity to stabilize my housing once more by utilizing my Veteran Monetary Benefits to the best of my ability.

Presently – Unemployed at the time of the writing of this book

I realized that I could use some more EMDR or Cognitive Behavioral Therapy (CBT) and had been encouraged to apply for social security disability to facilitate the treatments. I was denied twice,… even though I provided all my military medical documents that were signed by multiple Active Duty officer level medical doctors and Veterans Administration personnel dating back to 1991. This same medical evidence was severe enough to cause discharge from the armed forces, disrupt my ability to work / maintain gainful employment as noted in the charts on the previous pages,… yet another branch of the same governmental body of the United States denied that any of the medical evidence indicated disabling conditions.

In a letter dated March 31, 2011 and addressed to me,… the social security administration stated the following:

"We have determined your condition was not disabling on any date through 03/31/2008, when you were last insured for disability benefits. In deciding this, we considered the medical records, your statements, and how your condition affected your ability to work."

"In order to be entitled for benefits, your condition must be found to be severe prior to 03/31/2008, when you were last insured for disability benefits. The evidence in file is not sufficient to fully evaluate your claim and the evidence needed cannot be obtained. We have determined your condition was not disabling on any date through 03/31/2008, when you were last insured for disability benefits. In deciding this, we considered the medical records, your statements, and how your condition affected your ability to work."

"The evidence does not show that your condition was disabling on or before DLI 03/31/2008, the date that your Social Security Disability coverage ended."; Doctors and other trained staff looked at your case and made this decision. They work for your State but used our rules."

> *"Please remember that there are many types of disability programs, both government and private, which use different rules. A person may be receiving benefits under another program and still not be entitled under our rules. This may be true in your case."*

This news was a heavy blow as the second denial within one year and simply felt like another act of betrayal toward me,… from an authority type agency that I believed would be a safety net for me in the event of a situation like this one that I had found myself in. At this time I had creatively stretched my monthly Veterans Administration disability payments to purchase a small home which was critical to stabilizing my recovery process in terms of shelter, continued to pay student loans that could not be discharged in Bankruptcy court in 2004, food, heat, water, electric, pet care and other basic necessities such as car parts that I installed myself to cut operational costs for my nearly twenty years old 1995 Mazda MPV. This same car has served to haul all the many free landscape timbers, rocks, new free mulch from a tree trim service and even a lawnmower that I repaired after acquiring it off craigslist.com. I even used a portion of this money to pay for assembling a professional Book-Proposal to aid in the telling of my story that seems to be consistently summed up in one word,… BETRAYAL.

I am 49 years old in my fifth decade now and I had a night sweat the other night for the first time in approximately 12 – 24 months. I woke up out of a nightmare cold and with a soaking wet black "T"-shirt that I had been wearing. I simply did what I have always done,… rinsed my face with cold water, put on another dry shirt and returned to bed in an attempt to get back to rest. Because this pattern used to be an unrelenting nightly occurrence, it gives indication that I continue to improve at least in this regard. One night out of 365 – 730 is not bad. I have learned to be supportive of myself as best I can with the knowledge and skill that I have acquired. I often times do not know how to be "normal" in a regular way because I have spent 84% of my life thus far in a type of *strange-death* since age 8 and that has been my messed-up "normal". I have no children and have never been married,… I'm a family Man without a family.

My ideas coupled with the utilization of all this crap I have been through is much like a gardener would use manure to fertilize the soil carefully,… and specifically grow something of substance rather than random "weeds".

This book project has been a seed planted, geminated and rooted in a well fertilized soil,… we'll see what grows.

Epilogue

I thank you for taking the time to read and understand my silent story, a tale that may be indicative of a larger complex societal dilemma.

In December 2012, I began a brief, uneasy, re-establishment of communication with a few family members in regards to my potential Federal Drug Administration (FDA) approved treatments for PTSD at the http://SmartBrainAndHealth.com/ facility located in Santa Monica California.

During one brief phone call with my cousin Carver concerning his correct mailing address, the separation / severed family bond was intensely and awkwardly palpable within me and emotionally disturbing,… to say the least. It felt like we were meeting for the first time.

My Cousin is selling a family gun collection and my old drum set to raise money to help cover some of the associated costs. I've been selling items around my house also,… if it's not nailed down,… It's getting sold. My youngest sister Landy sent a check from the family for $2,000.00.

It is my expectation that the Transcranial-Magnetic-Stimulation (TMS), will advance my recovery just a little bit more and I will probably have a thirty (30) day treatment scheduled by May 2013.

I still have night-terrors but minus the sweats, shaking hands and muscle tension; moreover, they are very infrequent, for example, once per month rather than every night.

I still have random uncontrollable moments of vague impending doom daily, vivid intrusive memories and mostly without the skin tinkling sensation that plagued me for 41 years. The prickly skin feeling may happen one time out of every ten with a short duration of affect, diminished intensity, diminished body coverage such as just on my arms but nowhere else, non-repetitious triggering of subsequent responses from the initial event and without muscle tension. These changes / improvements have incrementally & gradually persisted during a seven year time period since my first EMDR treatment commenced in August 2005. I still continue to have my groceries and other items delivered as I have done for the past 9 years to avoid unnecessary environmental stimulus and pain (physical & mental); moreover, I believe this strategy has helped my system to recover in some way by reducing the overall stress on my nervous system.

I look forward to the TMS treatments getting to the core of my over-active / under-active brain areas and rectifying the problem at the source more accurately.

I did not follow through with the brain treatments.

I did however meet a wonderful woman and rediscovered love,… deep [within myself],… after the painful break-up of our relationship in Fall of 2013,… so much so that I was able to call my Mother on New-Years day 2014. For the first time in two years I spoke to her and told her that I love her and know that she and dad did their best when I was a child. My heart remains wide open today and I have not been able to locate the on-off valve of this "walk" through vulnerability. Not that I really want to turn it off. I find the connection to love to be a very empowering place to live from. A place of presence and choice in the moment that allows for the acceptance or rejection of anything, behavior or whatever,… all from a place of vulnerability.

Circumstances changed such that I chose not to initiate the TMS treatments four (4) years ago and I returned the $2,000.00 to Landy via check in 2014 after sorting out a financial mess due to a dissolved relationship in Florida.

In 2015 I called Mom on my 51st birthday as a present to myself. I was scared to breach the subject,…yet I told Mom in my best soft nervous voice that I loved her and that I had been hurting all these years since eight years old and that I had written a book about it. I told her that I had been mentally haunted by all the fighting between her and Dad. I told Mom that specifically the time when she almost stabbed me while attempting to stab Dad and then he put me in a head-lock. I told Mom that: "I forgive you and Dad". I told Mom that: "I know you did your best". Mom spoke in a soft low voice in response and Said: "I only wanted to scare your Dad". I said to Mom: "I understand Mom,… and I'm sure he was scared too",… "I was scared too Mom",… we both paused for a few seconds and then I changed the subject. I chose to let this be enough as reconciliation. I let this be the 51 year old Man giving the 8 year old child his voice in a respectful way to his 86 year old Mother. I realized that this must one of the toughest subjects for any Mother to have to contend with in terms of being confronted with the fact that She almost killed her own Son back then. The journey that I have been on in terms of sorting all this stuff out within my own mind and learning to have compassion toward myself and cut myself some slack, allowed me to see that these words were Moms' way of apologizing in the best way she could. So with tears in my eyes,… and a stable yet on the verge of cracking voice,… I said "I love you Mom",… she said: "I love you to",… call ended. The entire call lasted about 10 – 15 minutes but seemed like an hour. This was the shape of reconciliation between me and my Mother as a birthday gift to myself in 2015 at 51 years old. It took 43 years to get to that stage on my journey that you have read about in this book. For me,… it seems that Freedom, Vulnerability, Courage, Wisdom, Voice, Compassion and the learned willingness to embrace each of these characteristics,… have all materialized agonizingly slow,… one(1) letter at a time,… for each word,… over a period of 43 years. It took me 43 years to simply tell my Mom,… "I'm hurting Mom".

As of July 2017,… I have visited family in Knoxville three (3) times.

The first visit was due to the passing of my second oldest sister Mary J. Lovely.

Although in January I had announced my plans to return home for a visit, my personal time-table was altered by the death of my sister. I chose to fly home to Knoxville for the service and it was a bitter-sweet reunion after twenty (20) years of absence. To my "surprise",… I was welcomed with open arms and smiles to say the least! It was at this point that I profoundly realized in an odd twist of fate,… that I had become / been a thief. I had robbed many people of my presence,… especially my Nieces and Nephews,… many of whom are Great Nieces and Nephews. Nevertheless I both chose to leave,… and had to leave,… and stayed away in "pieces",… in order to later return somewhat put back together. While in Knoxville I had a sit-down talk with my sisters (4) and brother in-laws. I explained to them briefly what I desired to be done in the event of my passing. I told them about my recent chest pains that may be signs of impending heart trouble. I talked about how I couldn't have photos of family in my house because they tended to remind me of Mom and Dad fighting all those years ago. Except for the last night before flying back to Colorado, I spent the entire time bunked at my Mothers' apartment. The last night in town was spent at Francines' house.

I enjoyed spending time at my Brother in-laws' and Francines' house and their vegetable garden that was overrun with large tomatoes that my Brother in-law fried-up. My Brother still proudly uses my Dads' old roto-tiller from the 1970's…! At the dinner table we all were in such a hurry to gobble-up the green tomatoes that were positioned on my side of the table near me and my sister Landy that we almost ate all of them before my Brother in-law spoke up and said that he didn't get any. We looked at each other and went "ooops!",… with a smile on our face and puffed-out cheeks we had torn those bad-boys up. Brother got the last two fried green tomatoes. On a subsequent (third) visit in October 2017,… Brother in-law took me fishing in his bass boat out on Douglass Lake where he caught three(3) and I Caught one(1) largemouth. He taught me how to use a "popper" to attract the bass; moreover, I had never fished specifically for bass (Large or small mouth) before. Dad and I used to fish below the dam as a kid where we caught mostly channel-cat and Stripper Bass. Additionally,… in all the years (40 plus) that we've known each other we had never gone fishing together until now. It was fun speeding across the water at about 59 mph in his sleek 22 footer! That bad-boy will scoot with that Mercury 250hp motor…!!!

I spent time pulling weeds and watering Petie and Williams' vegetable garden during my first trip home also. It offered some spiritual "grounding" for me to put my hands in the soil and touch plants.

I visited one of my Nephews' houses just across the street from his Mother / my sister Petie. He too has a garden in his big backyard with a small orchard.

Moms' retirement village also has a large (100' x 30') vegetable garden. I saw eggplant, okra, tomato, peppers, squash, marigold, cucumber and dill but some of the other residents take care of it.

My first visit to Family in Knoxville in 20 years revealed some interesting imformation that I had often wondered about but since everything was always hush-hush,..it never came out until now.

It has only been recently brought to my attention this past July 2017 that I was not the only one whom witnessed the bullets / domestic violence between my Parents. I can only now imagine the potential mental anguish, pain and confusion that may have taken place within each of my siblings and brothers (in-laws). With this new information,… now more than ever before,… I realize that I have been in part,… a thief. I've robbed my entire Family and myself during the past 20 years of my estranged absence. I had thought that none of them cared about me,… yet they were simply grappling with their own personal perspectives of the situation(s). As we sat around the table on the backyard wooden deck at Francine and Melvins' house,…with tears in my eye I listened for the first time,… to each of my dear sisters recount their own horror stories. I had no clue that the similar scenarios that I had witnessed as a kid,… had played-out with such repetitiousness. Jeanie,… my eldest sister,…told of the time when she witnessed Mom and Dad arguing / fighting,…. and he picked Mom up over his shoulder and carried her off into the bed room. I must have not been at the house or it was before I was born,… or when I was extremely small (infant possibly). Because of what Jeanie told me that day,… I now potentially can conclude,… due to events that I will not disclose in this book,… that our parents' violent interactions witnessed by Jeanie as a young Lady could not have been the best visual training for my dear eldest Sister. I suspect that these "teachings" potentially forged ideas in her young mind; these ideas were not the best in terms of how a Man is to treat a Woman,…. nor what was,… or,… was not acceptable behavior. Petie,… my fourth eldest,… recounted a story of her and my Brother (in-law) witnessing the fighting and gun fire at our childhood house. Petie told me that it terribly frightened her and my Brother (in-law) so much so that he requested that she and he leave,… so as to not get mixed up in it. I've always thought of my Brothers as wise men,… and I realize now,… that was probably the wisest choice that he could have made,… in that situation,… from his perspective. Petie and William have been married for at least 46 years now since their teen years. Francine,… my fifth eldest sister recounted her horror story very similarly as my Brother (in law) Melvin sat silently with a look of horror on his face as if he was reliving the sadness all these years later. Francine told me of how her and Melvin were at our Ashland avenue home and also witnessed the fighting and gun fire between Mom and Dad. Once again I was not present for this incident and most likely was over at my Aunt Margarets' house where I tended to spend a lot of time during my early 1970's grade school years. Once more,… my ears heard the escape pattern of choice. Melvin and Francine chose to leave the house immediately,… and not get mixed up in Mom and Dads' violent choice of behavior. Two additional wise individuals whom have also been married about 46 years since their teen years,… and were high school sweethearts.

At the end of the day while modifying this epilog,… I have come to realize that this entire book and the subsequent perilous journey that it outlines,… has "simply" been about Courage, Vulnerability, Compassion and Open-Heartedness to some degree. My learned ability to "see" the frightened humanity in myself,… and all the other characters from the very start that is often times the unconscious / conscious conductor of our behavior. Even now,… in 2018,… each of us must choose to sit with our own brand of "suffering" in terms of what we did-do,… did-not-do,… or,… will-choose-to-do.

The twisted elements of:

1. Guilt (sensing that I failed at some arbitrary standard).
2. Shame (feeling that I'm not good enough based on some arbitrary standard).

3. Regret (concluding that my choices should have been different to get an alternative result presumably with a more favorable outcome).

Though it may appear as so in previous chapters,… I realize that this book is not an indictment of myself,… my family,… my parents,… my siblings, co-workers or community.

However it is my best attempt at this time,… to understand myself, my family-dynamic,… and to encourage my own individual internal healing at the very least.

On my wall,… behind my computer there is a saying printed,… "There is always a way to get there from here",… and beneath that saying I had scribbled the word "Imani" (faith). I glance at this quote every day at the beginning of my day,… and to me,… it also means to have faith in the unknown.

As of 29 July 2019 what has unfolded during the past 24 months of spending time around my family is a wonderful sense of welcoming punctuated with a palpable blatant uneasiness that gives me pause to my consideration to move back to Knoxville. It appears that there is a tremendous amount of generalized shame (elephant in the room) and guilting going on. This shaming is often verbalized toward other members of the family (Nieces & Nephews) and typically the younger (great Nieces and Nephews),…both indirectly and directly at times. I myself have often been yelled at,…or laughed at for caring about these younger family members that seem to repeatedly find themselves in difficult situations of their own doing or not. I've been even called a dummy for choosing to take [action],…. whether monetarily or otherwise to assist in sorting out a dilemma that is / has been typically presented to me. I've been told to stop worrying about these individuals,… by many family members. These requests suggest that I choose to simply stand by and allow younger members of the family to fall by the side of the "road" in plain sight without lifting a finger. I've been told that these individuals will not "listen". Some are in their 40's and a few are in their early 20's. As I observe this pattern and willingness by so many,…to seemly keep destructive secrets from one another and forsake other family members,…be it from emotional fatigue from past efforts to help said individuals,… or not,…..the invitation to re-join this [family] [pattern] is beyond my willingness to participate as an adult. I ask myself: "will I receive the same treatment?". Moreover,...my childhood was flooded with this type destructive activity,...that included my own unwitting participation with secret keeping. I have repeatedly addressed these patterns as the conversations have arose during the past 24 months,...and,...I have repeatedly encouraged my siblings to release the use of such behavior. I have repeatedly encouraged the awareness of the pattern(s) and the understanding that none of my Nieces and Nephews are inherently better nor worse than the other. Even if due to some specific behavior,... they all will succeed / slip-up as they go through life. Often times what's deemed "good" or "bad" gets used to demean / shame or belittle the individual family member(s) as a person,.. rather than acknowledge the specific choices that rendered the result / behavior. A result / behavior that may or may not be agreeable according to family "standards". It seems that the ideas of shaming, belittling, unhealthy secret keeping,.. and,... demeaning one another,... appear to be the go-to "standards" within the family structure that ultimately serve to undermine communication and learning. The ones that follow the dictate of the adults are often time praised. This type of unchallenged obedience can be a double-edged sword if accomplished to the detriment of the development of individual thinking and creativity. The potential stifling of the willingness to be vulnerable while fostering ingenuity and creativity within the family or elsewhere is at risk. I too was raised with an excessive obedient requirement,... of which I lived up to robotically and mindlessly. My behavior lead to me feeling forsaken as a child,...plus,...facilitated many of my challenges later in my life dealing with shame. I can not allow myself to choose to sacrifice all my personal mental health gains thus far,...simply to return to participating in a few old patterns of behavior as a quasi requirement to fit-in to the family that I love and care for deeply. Many members of my family may be suffering from emotional fatigue. This may have insidiously developed during the twenty years of my absence,.. while they have been consistently challenged with crisis after crisis,...daily in some cases,...monthly at the very least as I have come to understand it via observation within the past 24 months. With all this said,...there is a tremendous amount of talent and skill within my family and especially within the small business owner area historically and there is an individual that is currently considering a very courageous business venture and I can only wonder for now,… until I speak to her,….if any of what I have said above is of concern or impacts her choice as she considers her potential business venture.

In Imani,… I have written this letter to you,… my Nieces and Nephews.

I have faith that you will choose to keep your individual households void of domestic violence (physical, emotional, psychological) and full of joyful [voice] inspiring behavior.

At this time and in faith of a power greater than me,… I openly choose to allow my life to continue to unfold,… in all it's perfect-imperfection.

Imani.

Memoriam

Howard Lovely, Sr.
Ret. U.S. Army Sgt. FC
23 May 1929 – 24 Jan. 1994

Martha Leona Lovely (Jackson)
Oct. 13, 1929 – Oct. 6 2018

SISTERS:
Mary Joyce Lovely
30 Oct. 1952 – 11 July 2017

Sherry Ann Johnson (Lovely)
29 April 1954 - Jan. 1993

Aunt:
Charlene L Jackson
31 Mar. 1934 - 11 May 2017

Nephews:
Charles "Charlie" Herman Lovely
1970 - 29 April 1976

William Clifford Wilson, Jr.
2 Nov. 1972 - Jan. 1992

Byron Anthony Lovely
15 Aug. 1983 – 15 Jan. 2014

Neubern Paris "Punkine" Kelso, Jr.
25 May 1969 – 27 Jan. 2019

Cousins:
Carver Evers Lovely
26 Oct. 1963 - 10 Aug. 2017

Andrew Jackson
18 Mar. 1950 – 21 Feb. 2019
LGBTQ+

Brother In-law:
William Clifford Wilson, Sr.
8 April 1952 - 6 June 2019

Resources

National Suicide Prevention Life-Line 1-(800)273-Talk (8255)

EMDR Institute – Watsonville, CA 95077 (831)761-1040

Veterans Suicide Prevention Help-Line 1-(800)273-8255 (press 1)

http://helpguide.org

http://www.medicinenet.com

http://nami.org

http://www.makersofmemories.org/

LifeStyle Health Coach / Chef www.Joyfulivingforlife.org

Wellness Coach & Fitness Trainer
Tal Cohen - www.WowYourself.com
303-834-8938
303-330-2426 cell

Self-Awareness Courses Dr. Elsbeth Meuth & Freddy Zental Weaver - TantraNova Institute Chicago, IL 60618 www.tantraNova. com / (773)525-5006

Institute For Family Development
34004 16th Ave South, Suite 200
Federal Way, WA 98003-8903
(253) 874-3630 Seattle
(253) 927-1550 Tacoma
http://www.institutefamily.org

Military Mental Health Care
Resources and Referral
Direct Services / Health Benefits

TRICARE

(877) 874-2273 North Region

(800) 403-3950 South Region

(888) 874-9378 West Region

(888) 363-2273 Main TRICARE Information Service number

http://www.tricare.mil/mhshome.aspx **TRICARE** has three regional claims offices that can be contacted for information about healthcare benefits, including benefits for mental health and substance abuse services.

Deployment Health Clinical Center: www.pdhealth.mil/family.asp The Deployment Health Clinical Center Web site offers a list of resources for service members and their families and a link to the Department of Defense Mental Health Self-Assessment Program (alcohol and mental health screening).

Center for the Study of Traumatic Stress: http://www.cstsonline.org/

Defense and Veterans Brain Injury Center: http://www.dvbic.org

National Institute of Mental Health:
http://www.nimh.nih.gov/health/topics/post-traumatic-stress-disorder-ptsd/index.shtml

Afterdeployment.org: http://www.afterdeployment.org

Walter Reed Army Institute of Research – Psychiatry & Neurosciences: http://wrair-www.army.mil/Psychiatry-and-Neuroscience

Military Treatment Facility Locator: http://www.tricare.mil/mtf

Center for Deployment Psychology: http://www.deploymentpsych.org/

Department of Veterans Affairs: www.va.gov. The official Web site for the Department of Veterans Affairs offers information about benefits for returning veterans, those who have lost a loved one, health insurance information and facility locator to help find the closest VA Medical Center and the services it offers.

Vet Centers: www1.va.gov/directory/guide/vetcenter_flsh.asp Vet Centers provide readjustment counseling and outreach services to all veterans who served in any combat zone. Services are also available for their family members for military-related issues. Veterans have earned these benefits through their service and all are provided at no cost to the veteran or family. The 207 community based Vet Centers are located in all fifty states, District of Columbia, Guam, Puerto Rico and the US Virgin Islands. Use this link to locate your closest Vet Center.

National Center for PTSD: http://www.ncptsd.va.gov

Military OneSource
(800) 342-9647 (24-hour, toll-free number)
www.militaryonesource.com
• ARMY - "Army OneSource" 800-464-8107
• MARINES - "Marines OneSource" 800-869-0278
• NAVY - "Navy OneSource" 800-540-4123
• AIR FORCE - "Air Force OneSource" 800-707-5784
A Military OneSource consultant can provide a brief assessment and referral to mental health professionals across the country for six free counseling sessions.

Dept. of Defense Helpline: (800) 796-9699. This is a deployment helpline at Walter Reed Medical Center.

Homecoming

Veterans and Families: www.veteransandfamilies.org Veterans and Families provide information and resources to help homecoming Veterans and their families in their transition from military to civilian life. You will find links to online support groups.

Army Reserve Family Programs: www.arfp.org (800) 318-5298 (Army HR Command)
The Army Reserve Family Programs offers homecoming and reunion resources, including tips and links to resources.

National Guard Family Programs: www.guardfamily.org (888) 777-7731. The National Guard Family Programs offer information about programs, benefits, and resources, including family, youth and community outreach initiatives.

Iraq and Afghanistan Veterans of America: www.iava.org/index.php. The Iraq and Afghanistan Veterans of America provides support through advocacy, education and fundraising (fundraising mainly for VA hospitals).

National Veterans Foundation: www.nvf.org (888) 777-4443 (hotline) (9am-9pm PST). The National Veterans Foundation is operated by veterans and helps veterans and families access the help they need, including suicide and crisis intervention and mental health/PTSD counseling.

Wounded Soldier Support

Military Severely Injured Joint Operations Center: /www.militaryonesource.com (888) 774-1361 (24-hour hotline). This Center offers assistance for severely wounded service members and their families by connecting them with various military and government agencies. They offer help with medical care, rehabilitation, education, employment, mental health counseling, and financial assistance and accommodation issues. They also offer regional ombudsmen/advocates. The Center is staffed with registered nurses, master's level researchers and counselors working as care managers who can answer questions and provide nationwide assistance.

National Amputation Foundation: www.nationalamputation.org (516) 887-3600. This organization provides support for recent amputees, including in person peer support and phone support. They also offer donated medical equipment and printed information.

Loss of a Family Member

American Gold Star Mothers: www.goldstarmoms.com (202) 265-0991. They are a non-profit membership organization for mothers who have lost a son or daughter in the military. They provide support and sponsor memorial programs and events.

TAPS (Tragedy Assistance Program for Survivors): www.taps.org (202) 588-TAPS (8277).
TAPS offers support for survivors: peer support as well as 24-hour crisis intervention. They also provide information about benefits and other services, survivor seminars, camps for children and have an online chat.

VA/DoD Clinical Practice Guidelines: http://www.healthquality.va.gov/

Post-Deployment Health Evaluation and Management (PDH-CPG)

Management of Major Depressive Disorder in Adults (MDD-CPG)

Management of Medically Unexplained Symptoms (MUS-CPG): Chronic Pain and Fatigue

Management of Post-Traumatic Stress Disorders (PTSD-CPG)

Rehabilitation of Lower Limb Amputation (AMP-CPG)

Management of Concussion/mild Traumatic Brain Injury (mTBI CPG)

Management of Substance Use Disorder (SUD)

EMDR Related Resources

EMDR Institute: www.emdr.com. General information about EMDR, contact information for EMDR therapists by area, summary of EMDR research, information on subscribing to general EMDR internet discussion list & order forms for EMDR books

EMDR International Association: www.emdria.org Training standards for certification and approved consultant status. Contact information for approved consultants by area. Information on annual conference, schedule of EMDRIA-approved workshops, and instructions for subscribing to military SIG internet discussion list (members only)

EMDR Humanitarian Assistance Programs: www.emdrhap.org Nonprofit-Information on pro-bono training programs. Order forms for EMDR books, pamphlets and treatment aids

NEUROTEK Corporation www.neurotekcorp.com Information on ordering light-bars, lap-scans, tactile and audio-scans

www.ingramcontent.com/pod-product-compliance
Lightning Source LLC
Chambersburg PA
CBHW021138260726
48656CB00023B/462